ALL ONE IN CHRIST

EDWARD FESER

All One in Christ

A Catholic Critique of Racism
and Critical Race Theory

IGNATIUS PRESS   SAN FRANCISCO

Cover photograph ©iStock

Cover design by Enrique J. Aguilar

© 2022 by Ignatius Press, San Francisco
All rights reserved
ISBN 978-1-62164-580-1 (PB)
ISBN 978-1-64229-242-8 (eBook)
Library of Congress Control Number 2021952109
Printed in the United States of America ∞

CONTENTS

Church Teaching against Racism

Racism is widely, and rightly, condemned today. Indeed, in a world that seems increasingly divided on moral and political issues, that racism is wrong is one of the few things about which there appears to be broad agreement. But what exactly is racism, and why is it wrong? What does the Catholic Church teach on the subject? What does she teach regarding other issues that often arise in discussions of racism, such as slavery, immigration, and nationalism? What should Catholics think about Critical Race Theory and other increasingly influential ideas and movements promoted in the name of antiracism? This book addresses these questions.

In his 1971 apostolic letter *Octogesima Adveniens*, Pope Saint Paul VI condemned what he referred to as "racialist prejudice", and affirmed:

> The members of mankind share the same basic rights and duties, as well as the same supernatural destiny. Within a country which belongs to each

> one, all should be equal before the law, find equal
> admittance to economic, cultural, civic and social
> life and benefit from a fair sharing of the nation's
> riches. (16)

This suggests a useful definition of racism, which is best understood as the denial of what the pope here affirms. In other words, racism is the belief that not all races have the same basic rights and duties and/ or supernatural destiny and, therefore, not all races should be equal before the law, find equal admittance to economic, cultural, civic, and social life, or benefit from a fair sharing of the nation's riches. Racism thus entails giving some races special favor over others in these respects.

The Church has consistently condemned racism in this sense and did so with special emphasis during the twentieth century. In his 1914 encyclical *Ad Beatissimi Apostolorum*, Pope Benedict XV lamented:

> Being as it were compacted and fitly joined
> together in one body, we should love one another,
> with a love like that which one member bears to
> another in the same body.... But in reality never
> was there less brotherly activity amongst men than
> at the present moment. Race hatred has reached its
> climax; peoples are more divided by jealousies than
> by frontiers. (6–7)

Condemning developments in Nazi Germany in his 1937 encyclical *Mit Brennender Sorge*, Pope Pius XI wrote:

Whoever exalts race, or the people ... or any other fundamental value of the human community—however necessary and honorable be their function in worldly things—whoever raises these notions above their standard value and divinizes them to an idolatrous level, distorts and perverts an order of the world planned and created by God. (8)

In *Pacem in Terris*, Pope Saint John XXIII called for "the elimination of every trace of racial discrimination" on the grounds that "no one can be by nature superior to his fellows, since all men are equally noble in natural dignity" (86, 89). The Second Vatican Council, in the declaration *Nostra Aetate*, taught:

The Church reproves, as foreign to the mind of Christ, any discrimination against men or harassment of them because of their race, color, condition of life, or religion. On the contrary, following in the footsteps of the holy Apostles Peter and Paul, this sacred synod ardently implores the Christian faithful to "maintain good fellowship among the nations" (1 Pet 2:12), and, if possible, to live for their part in peace with all men, so that they may truly be sons of the Father who is in heaven. (5)

The 1988 document *The Church and Racism: Towards a More Fraternal Society*, issued by the Pontifical Commission on Justice and Peace at the direction of Pope Saint John Paul II, observes:

Racial prejudice or racist behavior continues to trouble relations between persons, human groups

and nations. Public opinion is increasingly incensed
by it. Moral conscience can by no means accept it.
The Church is especially sensitive to this discriminatory attitude. The message which she has drawn
from biblical Revelation strongly affirms the dignity of every person created in God's image, the
unity of humankind in the Creator's plan, and
the dynamics of the reconciliation worked by
Christ the Redeemer who has broken down the
dividing wall which kept opposing worlds apart in
order to recapitulate all persons in him. (1)

The *Compendium of the Social Doctrine of the Church*,
also issued during the pontificate of John Paul II,
sums up the Church's condemnation of racism,
which is grounded in her understanding of both
human nature and the demands of the Gospel:

> *"God shows no partiality" (Acts 10:34; cf. Rom 2:11;*
> *Gal 2:6; Eph 6:9), since all people have the same dig-*
> *nity as creatures made in his image and likeness.* The
> Incarnation of the Son of God shows the equality
> of all people with regard to dignity: "There is nei-
> ther Jew nor Greek, there is neither slave nor free,
> there is neither male nor female; for you are all one
> in Christ Jesus" (Gal 3:28; cf. Rom 10:12; 1 Cor
> 12:13, Col 3:11).
>
> *Since something of the glory of God shines on the*
> *face of every person, the dignity of every person before*
> *God is the basis of the dignity of man before other men.*
> Moreover, this is the ultimate foundation of the
> radical equality and brotherhood among all people,

regardless of their race, nation, sex, origin, culture, or class.[1]

This twofold foundation of the Church's condemnation of racism—in nature and grace, in our common origin and our supernatural destiny—requires special emphasis and comment, for it differs crucially from the approach taken in many secular discussions of racism.

Defenders of racism commonly posit racial differences of a cognitive, affective, or behavioral sort that they claim are grounded in genetics or other biological factors. Their critics respond that the scientific evidence for such claims is weak. But from the point of view of Catholic theology, to address the issue at this level alone would be superficial. The Church's condemnation of racism is grounded in considerations about human nature that go deeper than anything that could be either discovered or undermined by biological science. As the document *The Church and Racism* judges:

> The sciences, on their part, contribute to dispelling much of the false evidence used to justify racist behavior.... But the sciences are not sufficient to substantiate anti-racist convictions. Because of their methods, they do not allow themselves to say the last word about the human person and his or her

[1] Pontifical Council for Justice and Peace, *Compendium of the Social Doctrine of the Church*, no. 144. Hereafter, *Compendium*.

destiny, and to define universal moral rules of a
binding nature for consciences. (18)

For the Church, the source of our common dignity
is primarily to be found, not in the *body* as understood by science, but in the *soul*—which, as the *Catechism of the Catholic Church* teaches, "refers to the
innermost aspect of man, that which is of greatest
value in him, that by which he is most especially
in God's image: 'soul' signifies the *spiritual principle* in
man" (363).[2] Being spiritual, this principle cannot
be detected at the genetic or any other biological
level of description, and indeed it is not the product
of biological processes. The *Catechism* continues:

> The Church teaches that every spiritual soul is cre-
> ated immediately by God—it is not "produced"
> by the parents—and also that it is immortal: it
> does not perish when it separates from the body at
> death, and it will be reunited with the body at the
> final Resurrection. (366)[3]

Now, as Saint Thomas Aquinas teaches, our souls
are what give us human beings that feature which
distinguishes us from the other animals—our *rationality*, which is manifest in our capacities to know or
understand, and to will or choose.[4] And the highest

[2] Cf. 1 Cor 6:19–20; 15:44–45.

[3] Cf. Pius XII, *Humani Generis*: DS 3896; Paul VI, *CPG* §8; Lateran
Council V (1513): DS 1440.

[4] Thomas Aquinas, *Summa Theologiae*, trans. Fathers of the English
Dominican Province (New York: Benziger Bros., 1948), 1.76.3.
Hereafter, *ST*.

exercise of these capacities is to know and to love *God*. Aquinas writes:

> Augustine says (Gen. ad lit. vi, 12): "Man's excellence consists in the fact that God made him to His own image by giving him an intellectual soul, which raises him above the beasts of the field."[5]

> Since man is said to be the image of God by reason of his intellectual nature, he is the most perfectly like God according to that in which he can best imitate God in his intellectual nature. Now the intellectual nature imitates God chiefly in this, that God understands and loves Himself.[6]

Knowing and loving God, then, are for Saint Thomas the fullest way in which we manifest our dignity and nature as made in the divine image. The *Catechism* concurs with this judgment:

> Of all visible creatures only man is "able to know and love his creator." He is "the only creature on earth that God has willed for its own sake," and he alone is called to share, by knowledge and love, in God's own life. It was for this end that he was created, and this is the fundamental reason for his dignity. (356)[7]

To be sure, this common human nature, and in particular our capacity to come to know and love

[5] *ST* I.93.2,4.

[6] *ST* I.93.4,3.

[7] Vatican Council II, Pastoral Constitution on the Church in the Modern World *Gaudium et Spes* (December 7, 1965), 12§3; 24§3. Hereafter, *GS*.

God, has been damaged by original sin. But this damage has been suffered by all human beings, of every race. As Saint Paul teaches, "All have sinned and fall short of the glory of God" and "sin came into the world through one man and death through sin, and so death spread to all men because all men sinned" (Rom 3:23; 5:12). That brings us to the second ground of our dignity, which is *super*natural— that is to say, deriving from a source beyond our nature—and thus afforded to us only by grace. The sin and death that afflicts all human beings is remedied for all human beings by Christ's death and Resurrection. For "he died for all" (2 Cor 5:15), so that "as one man's trespass led to condemnation for all men, so one man's act of righteousness leads to acquittal and life for all men" (Rom 5:18); and "as in Adam all die, so also in Christ shall all be made alive" (1 Cor 15:22). Hence, just as all races share the same human nature inherited from Adam, so too are they all offered the same grace through Christ. As Saint Paul famously writes:

> For in Christ Jesus you are all sons of God, through faith. For as many of you as were baptized into Christ have put on Christ. There is neither Jew nor Greek, there is neither slave nor free, there is neither male nor female; for you are all one in Christ Jesus. (Gal 3:26–28)

In sum, our basic rights and obligations under natural law are grounded in our nature as rational creatures capable of understanding and free choice, and thus of knowing and loving God. This nature, and thus these rights and obligations, are the same for all human beings, of whatever race. Our basic rights and obligations as potential citizens of heaven are grounded in grace. This grace has been offered to all human beings, of whatever race. Hence, whatever biological and cultural differences may exist between the races, nature and grace alike ensure that their basic rights and duties are the same. This is the deep and unshakable foundation for the Church's condemnation of racism. The Second Vatican Council's pastoral constitution *Gaudium et Spes* summarizes this teaching as follows:

> Since all men possess a rational soul and are created in God's likeness, since they have the same nature and origin, have been redeemed by Christ and enjoy the same divine calling and destiny, the basic equality of all must receive increasingly greater recognition.
>
> True, all men are not alike from the point of view of varying physical power and the diversity of intellectual and moral resources. Nevertheless, with respect to the fundamental rights of the person, every type of discrimination, whether social or cultural, whether based on sex, race, color, social condition, language or religion, is to be overcome and eradicated as contrary to God's intent. (29)

2

Late Scholastics and Early Modern Popes against Slavery

The Church's condemnation of racism is neither a recent novelty nor a matter of her following the lead of secular moral attitudes. On the contrary, she has taught the same thing for centuries, and long before the rise of the contemporary secular consensus against racism. Now, as *The Church and Racism* observes, racism is largely a modern phenomenon:

> Historically, racial prejudice, in the strict sense of the word—that is, awareness of the biologically determined superiority of one's own race or ethnic group with respect to others—developed above all from the practice of colonization and slavery at the dawn of the modern era....
>
> Greco-Roman antiquity, for example, does not seem to have known racial myths. If the Greeks were convinced of the cultural superiority of their civilization, they did not, by the same token, consider

the so-called "barbarians" inferior because of innate biological reasons....

The Hebrew people, as the Books of the Old Testament testify, were aware to a unique degree of God's love for them, manifested in the form of a gratuitous covenant with him... The place of other peoples in salvation history was not always clearly understood in the beginning, and these other peoples were at times even stigmatized in prophetic preaching to the degree that they remained attached to idolatry. They were not, however, the object of disparagement or of a divine curse because of their ethnic diversity. The criterion of distinction was religious.[1]

It is "with the discovery of the New World", the document notes, that "attitudes changed", as European soldiers and traders reduced the Indians of the Americas and black Africans to slavery and "began to develop a racist theory in order to justify their actions". The Church immediately condemned this development in the harshest terms possible. For example, in his 1537 bull *Sublimis Deus*, Pope Paul III taught:

Christ, who is the Truth itself, that has never failed and can never fail, said to the preachers of the faith whom He chose for that office "Go ye and teach

[1] Pontifical Commission on Justice and Peace, *The Church and Racism: Towards a More Fraternal Society* (Vatican City: Pontificia Commissio Iustitia et Pax, 1988), no. 2.

all nations." He said all, without exception, for all are capable of receiving the doctrines of the faith.

The enemy of the human race, who opposes all good deeds in order to bring men to destruction, beholding and envying this, invented a means never before heard of, by which he might hinder the preaching of God's word of Salvation to the people: he inspired his satellites who, to please him, have not hesitated to publish abroad that the Indians of the West and the South, and other people of whom We have recent knowledge should be treated as dumb brutes created for our service, pretending that they are incapable of receiving the catholic faith.

We, who, though unworthy, exercise on earth the power of our Lord and seek with all our might to bring those sheep of His flock who are outside into the fold committed to our charge, consider, however, that the Indians are truly men and that they are not only capable of understanding the catholic faith but, according to our information, they desire exceedingly to receive it. Desiring to provide ample remedy for these evils, We define and declare ... that, notwithstanding whatever may have been or may be said to the contrary, the said Indians and all other people who may later be discovered by Christians, are by no means to be deprived of their liberty or the possession of their property, even though they be outside the faith of Jesus Christ; and that they may and should, freely and legitimately, enjoy their liberty and the possession of their property; nor should they be in any

way enslaved; should the contrary happen, it shall
be null and have no effect.[2]

Note that in this document from *five centuries ago*,
the pope characterizes as nothing less than *satanic*
the treatment of Indians and other human beings
as if they were mere brute beasts and teaches in a
definitive way (he "defines and declares") that they
must not be deprived of their liberty or property.
It is true that this teaching was widely ignored by
those who colonized the New World. But *that was
the Church's teaching*, centuries before antiracism
became a standard cause among secularists and
liberals—indeed, centuries before the phenomena
of secularism and liberalism existed.

Though there were Catholic thinkers at the time
who resisted this teaching, some of the great Scholastic theologians of the day upheld it and hammered
out its intellectual foundations. Especially important
in this connection are Francisco de Vitoria (c. 1486–
1546) and Bartoloméo de Las Casas (1474–1566).[3]

[2] Found in Francis Augustus MacNutt, *Batholomew de Las Casas: His
Life, His Apostolate, and His Writings* (Cleveland: A.H. Clark, 1909),
427–29. Internet Archive, https://archive.org/details/bartholome
wdelaoomacn/page/426/mode/2up?q=enemy.

[3] Francisco de Vitoria, "On the American Indians", in *Political Writings*, ed. Anthony Pagden and Jeremy Lawrence (Cambridge: Cambridge University Press, 1991); Bartolomé de Las Casas, *A Short Account
of the Destruction of the Indies* (New York: Penguin Books, 1992). A
useful overview of their views can be found in Brian Tierney, *The
Idea of Natural Rights* (Grand Rapids, Mich.: William B. Eerdmans

Vitoria addressed four reasons why some in his day claimed, or might have claimed, that the Indians of the Americas lacked the basic rights that other human beings have: (1) they were sinners, (2) they were infidels, (3) they lacked rationality, or (4) they lacked sufficient intelligence. Vitoria disposed of each of these arguments.

First, he pointed out that natural rights are grounded in human nature and that sinners and infidels have the same human nature as everyone else. Hence, they have the same basic rights as everyone else (such as the right not to be murdered, the right not to be stolen from, and so on). Hence, whether the American Indians were sinners or nonbelievers is irrelevant to their having natural rights, and thus no one could justify treating them as if they did not have them.

As to the claim that the American Indians lacked rationality, Vitoria pointed out that this is obviously false given that they had customs and institutions that only creatures with reason have (laws, the institution of marriage, cities, etc.). He also argued that it will not do to suggest that they somehow had only the *potential* for rationality, without having actually realized that potential; this, he held, would

---

Publishing Company, 2001), chap. 11. Cf. John Eppstein, *The Catholic Tradition of the Law of Nations* (London: Burns, Oates, and Washbourne, 1935), chap. 15.

violate the principle of Scholastic philosophy that nature does nothing in vain. Vitoria's point seems to be that it makes no sense to suppose that a large and ongoing population of human beings would have only the potential for rationality without ever actualizing it, because in that case their possession of the potential would be pointless, which violates the said Scholastic principle. If a population really has the potential for rationality, then over time and across the population that potential is inevitably going to be realized.

In response to the claim that the Indians lacked sufficient intelligence, Vitoria says that though children and mentally ill people lack the intelligence others have, they do not lack basic human rights, because they have the same human nature as everyone else. Hence, Vitoria concludes, claims to the effect that the Indians lacked the same mental acuity as the Spaniards could not justify denying that they had the same natural rights.

The ancient Greek philosopher Aristotle had notoriously defended the thesis that some people are naturally fit only to serve others, and Vitoria responded to the view that this thesis could be used to justify enslaving the Indians. He argued that this conclusion is ruled out by the circumstance that even the servile persons described by Aristotle have the same rational nature as every other human being, so that they have the same natural rights as other human beings. Hence, even someone better suited to serve others could not justly be treated as property or otherwise less than human.

Las Casas was even more thoroughgoing and passionate in his defense of the rights and equal dignity of the Indians of the Americas. He argued strongly against any suggestion that the Indians were morally or intellectually inferior to Spaniards, and he put special emphasis on the rights to personal liberty and government by consent. Fellow rational creatures, he insisted, have to be appealed to via rational persuasion rather than force. He also emphasized the brotherhood of man both on Christian and natural law grounds, writing: "All the peoples of the world are humans and there is only one definition of all humans and of each one, that is that they are rational.... Thus all the races of humankind are one."[4]

Las Casas developed an especially important argument against any suggestion that Aristotle's view that some people are naturally servile could be used to justify racial slavery. First, he noted some problems with claims, common in his day, to the effect that some peoples were "barbarian" races. What does that mean, exactly? In the original sense of the term, "barbarian" peoples were those whose language was strange, but in this trivial sense *all* people are "barbarian" relative to those

[4] Quoted in Tierney, *The Idea of Natural Rights*, 273.

who speak a different language. In another sense, a "barbarian" people is one that is especially cruel, but in this sense, Las Casas points out, the *Spanish* could be said to be barbarians given their treatment of the Indians. In yet another sense, "barbarians" referred to non-Christian peoples. But the pagan Greeks and Romans were non-Christians, and yet they were not considered by Christian writers to have been barbarians.

Las Casas argues that a "barbarian", in the only interesting sense of the term, would be someone who essentially lived the life of a savage, bereft of reason and barely above the level of nonhuman animals, like a proverbial forest-dwelling "wild man". He would for that reason essentially be a damaged human being, his defects of rationality comparable to blindness or lameness. But here Las Casas makes two key points. First, he says, even such a person would still be a human being (even if his use of reason was greatly stunted) and would therefore retain the basic human rights.

Second, he argues, such people would also in the nature of the case be extremely rare and isolated. There could not, in principle, be a *race* of barbarians in this sense, for it simply makes no sense for there to be a race of people who have the basic powers of rationality that other human beings have, with all the moral duties under natural law which that entails, and yet, generation after generation, are always fundamentally stunted or crippled in their capacity to use those powers. They would be like a race of people who, generation after generation, are always born blind or crippled. There would be a kind of *perversity* in such a scenario that would violate the Scholastic principle that nature does nothing in vain. (Here, Las Casas essentially extends the line of argument that Vitoria proposed.)

What Vitoria and Las Casas developed, then, are lines of argument that, on grounds of Scholastic philosophy, rule out the very possibility of a race that is naturally inferior to others. And thus they rule out any justification for racism in the sense condemned by the Church from Pope Paul III down to the present. Later Scholastic thinkers such as Francisco Suárez (1548–1617) reiterated this line of thought,[5] and it became standard in Catholic philosophy and theology.

Some will ask: But didn't the Catholic Church once defend slavery of the kind that Vitoria and Las Cases criticized, and precisely on natural law grounds? The answer is no, she did not. To be sure, and as has already been mentioned, there were individual Catholic writers who defended racial slavery, though their position died out and the views of thinkers like Vitoria and Las Casas prevailed.

[5] John P. Doyle, "Francisco Suárez: On Preaching the Gospel to People like the American Indians", *Fordham International Law Journal* 15 (1991): 879–951.

But it is not true that the Church as an institution defended slavery of that kind.

It must be kept in mind that the word "slavery" is ambiguous. What we usually think of when we hear the term today is *chattel* slavery of the kind practiced in the United States before the Civil War, which involved the complete ownership of another person as if he were an animal or an inanimate object, and where the person is innocent of any crime and has been stripped of his liberty involuntarily. This is always and intrinsically evil, and the Church has never defended it. There are, however, other practices that were sometimes loosely labeled "slavery" but are very different from chattel slavery. For example, there is *indentured servitude*, which is a contract to give the right to one's labor to another person for a prolonged period of time—for example, in payment of a debt. And there is *penal servitude*, which involves forcing someone to labor as part of a punishment for a crime. Indentured servitude is essentially an extreme version of an ordinary labor contract, and penal servitude is an extension of the loss of liberty a justly punished prisoner is already sentenced to endure.

Catholic theologians have long regarded such practices as so morally hazardous, and, in particular, as posing a serious enough danger of degenerating into chattel slavery, that in practice they ought not to be employed. But it is practices of these kinds (rather than chattel slavery) that the Church did not condemn as intrinsically immoral. Regarding the modern slave trade and the practice of chattel slavery, the Church and the popes have, in fact, consistently condemned them, beginning at least as far back as the fifteenth century.[6] For example, in the 1435 bull *Sicut Dudum*, Pope Eugene IV condemned the enslavement of the peoples of the newly colonized Canary Islands. We have already seen that Pope Paul III condemned the enslavement of the American Indians and others in 1537 in *Sublimis Deus*, and in another document (*Pastorale Officium*) he attached a penalty of excommunication to such mistreatment.[7] In the 1591 bull *Cum Sicuti*, Pope Gregory XIV condemned the enslavement of the Indians of the Philippines, also attaching to this crime a penalty of excommunication.

In his 1639 bull *Commissum Nobis*, Pope Urban VIII reaffirmed the teaching of Pope Paul III against the enslavement of the Indians, including the penalty of excommunication. In 1686, under Blessed Pope Innocent XI, the Congregation of the Holy Office condemned the chattel enslavement of black

[6] Joel S. Panzer, *The Popes and Slavery* (New York: Alba House, 1996), and Eppstein, *The Catholic Tradition*, chap. 15.

[7] To be sure, *Pastorale Officium* was retracted by the pope for political reasons the following year, but as Panzer points out, its penalty of excommunication was restored by Pope Paul's successors beginning with Urban VIII. *The Popes and Slavery*, 33; 65–66.

Africans and taught that those who had been so enslaved must be freed and compensated by those involved in enslaving them. In 1741, in *Immensa Pastorum*, Pope Benedict XIV complained that some in Brazil were disobeying the prohibitions against enslaving the Indians that had been issued by his predecessors. He reiterated the teaching of Paul III and Urban VIII, and extended the penalty of excommunication even to those who dared to dissent from their teaching.

Pope Gregory XVI, in the 1839 document *In Supremo*, condemned the continued enslavement of Indians and blacks and strictly prohibited any dissent, public or private, in teaching or in writing, from the Church's teaching on the subject.[8] An 1866 Instruction from the Holy Office under Blessed Pope Pius IX, while permitting servitude of the kinds mentioned earlier (such as indentured servitude and penal servitude), does not permit the enslavement of someone who has been "unjustly deprived of his liberty" and affirmed the right of such a slave to flee.[9] In 1888 in *In Plurimis*, Pope

[8] It is sometimes alleged that Gregory was condemning only the slave trade and not slavery itself, but as Panzer shows, this is clearly not the case. For example, Gregory warns that "no one in the future dare to bother unjustly, despoil their possessions, or reduce to slavery Indians, Blacks, or other such peoples." *The Popes and Slavery*, 46–48.

[9] As Panzer notes, while it is regrettable that this Instruction from the Holy Office was insufficiently sensitive to the grave moral hazards of indentured servitude, penal servitude, and the like, it would be

Leo XIII hailed the abolition of slavery in Brazil and reviewed his predecessors' teaching on the subject, and in *Catholicae Ecclesiae* in 1890 he grounded the Church's opposition to slavery in the common origin of all human beings as well as in their common call to salvation.

Hence, when the Second Vatican Council condemned slavery in the 1965 pastoral constitution *Gaudium et Spes*, this was not some novelty or a matter of the Church catching up with enlightened secular morality. On the contrary, it was simply a continuation of what the Church had already been teaching consistently for over five centuries.[10]

---

intellectually dishonest to ignore the distinction between these forms of servitude and the chattel slavery that the Church has consistently condemned, and to pretend that the Instruction permitted the latter. Ibid., 55–56.

[10] Sometimes Pope Nicholas V's 1452 bull *Dum Diversas* is alleged to teach the legitimacy of chattel slavery. But that is not the case. What Nicholas was permitting there was penal servitude as punishment for an enemy in a just war. Certainly this is regrettable, but it is not inconsistent with the letter (even if it sits poorly with the spirit) of the teaching of Nicholas' predecessor Eugene IV and his successors Paul III, Gregory XIV, Urban VIII, et al. For a discussion of *Dum Diversas*, see Richard Raiswell, "Nicholas V, Papal Bulls of", in Junius P. Rodriguez, ed., *The Historical Encyclopedia of World Slavery*, vol. 2 (Santa Barbara, Calif.: ABC-CLIO, 1997), 469.

3

The Rights and Duties
of Nations and Immigrants

The Church's teaching against racism is unambiguous, deeply rooted in her theology, and has been consistently reiterated in her tradition. She has no need for instruction on the subject from the modern secular world. As Pope Pius XI wrote in *Divini Redemptoris*:

> The enemies of the Church ... accuse her of having failed to act in conformity with her principles, and from this conclude to the necessity of seeking other solutions. The utter falseness and injustice of this accusation is shown by the whole history of Christianity. To refer only to a single typical trait, it was Christianity that first affirmed the real and universal brotherhood of all men of whatever race and condition. This doctrine she proclaimed by a method, and with an amplitude and conviction, unknown to preceding centuries; and with it she potently contributed to the abolition of slavery. (36)

If anything, it is the teaching of the Church that provides a corrective to the superficiality of much contemporary secular thinking on the subject of racism.

One respect in which this is true has to do with questions about national loyalties and immigration. In contemporary social and political debate, accusations of racism are routinely leveled against anyone who argues for preserving the religious, cultural, and linguistic heritage of a nation in the interests of preserving its national identity, especially if this is conjoined with concern about large influxes of immigrants or immigrants who enter a country illegally. Of course, racist attitudes can inspire hostility to immigrants and excessive devotion to one's nation. However, it would be gravely unjust and uncharitable reflexively to attribute *all* concerns about national identity and immigration to racism. Moreover, it would be contrary to the clear and consistent teaching of the Church.

The Church has always recognized that a special attachment to one's nation and its culture is by no means an irrational prejudice. On the contrary, it is natural to us, an extension of our innate attachment to family. Saint Thomas Aquinas teaches that patriotism is a moral virtue and an extension of the piety we owe our parents.[1] Likewise, the *Catechism of the Catholic Church* teaches that the fourth

[1] *ST* II-II.101.1.

commandment, which commands us to honor our mothers and fathers, "extends to the duties of ... citizens to their country, and to those who administer or govern it" (2199), and that "the love and service of *one's country* follow from the duty of gratitude and belong to the order of charity" (2239).

In his book *Memory and Identity*, Pope Saint John Paul II noted that citizens of modern Western European countries often have "reservations" about the notion of "national identity as expressed through culture", and have even "arrived at a stage which could be defined as 'post-identity'."[2] There is "a widespread tendency to move toward supranational structures, even internationalism" with "small nations ... allow[ing] themselves to be absorbed into larger political structures"[3] However, the pope noted, the disappearance of the nation would be contrary to the natural order of things as understood by the Church:

> Yet it still seems that nation and native land, like the family, are permanent realities. In this regard, Catholic social doctrine speaks of "natural" societies, indicating that both the family and the nation have a particular bond with human nature, which has a social dimension. Every society's formation takes place in and through the family: of this there

---

[2] John Paul II, *Memory and Identity* (New York: Rizzoli, 2005), 86.
[3] Ibid., 66.

can be no doubt. Yet something similar could also be said about the nation.[4]

In particular, says the pope, the nation and the cultural heritage that defines it cannot be replaced by mere political institutions or legal ties between people:

> The term "nation" designates a community based in a given territory and distinguished from other nations by its culture. Catholic social doctrine holds that the family and the nation are both natural societies, not the product of mere convention. Therefore, in human history they cannot be replaced by anything else. For example, the nation cannot be replaced by the State, even though the nation tends naturally to establish itself as a State.... Still less is it possible to identify the nation with so-called democratic society, since here it is a case of two distinct, albeit interconnected orders. Democratic society is closer to the State than is the nation. Yet the nation is the ground on which the State is born.[5]

Since, as the *Catechism* teaches, "every human community needs an authority to govern it" (1898), the authority of the State is a natural concomitant of the human community that is the nation. As John Paul says, "The nation must exist as a State."[6] And as

---

[4] Ibid., 67.

[5] Ibid., 69–70.

[6] Ibid., 70. Here the pope is quoting approvingly a remark of Stanislaw Wyspianski.

he goes on to say, "The issue of democracy comes later, in the arena of [the] internal politics" of the State.[7] Hence, since the nation is the natural foundation on which the State and democracy are built, they can hardly exist without it, any more than a household can exist without a house's foundation.

Thus, patriotic attachment remains, today no less than in the past, something to which one's nation has a right. The pope writes:

> If we ask where patriotism appears in the Decalogue, the reply comes without hesitation: it is covered by the fourth commandment, which obliges us to honor our father and mother. It is included under the umbrella of the Latin word *pietas*, which underlines the religious dimension of the respect and veneration due to parents....
>
> Patriotism is a love for everything to do with our native land: its history, its traditions, its language, its natural features. It is a love which extends also to the works of our compatriots and the fruits of their genius. Every danger that threatens the overall good of our native land becomes an occasion to demonstrate this love.[8]

Like all affections, love of country can become excessive, to the point of arrogance toward other nations or even idolatry. "Nationalism" is the label

[7] Ibid.
[8] Ibid., 65–66.

usually attached to such a disordered love of country (though it is important to note that sometimes this word is used in a more innocent way, as a synonym for "patriotism"). The Church warns against such excess. In *Populorum Progressio*, Pope Saint Paul VI condemned the "haughty pride" of a nationalism which would exclude "love for the whole family of man" (62), and in *Mit Brennender Sorge*, Pope Pius XI condemned the diabolical nationalism of Nazi Germany. But virtues are means between extremes, and just as one can show too much attachment to one's nation, so too can one show too little. Patriotism is the sober middle ground, and those who eschew it in the name of cosmopolitanism or internationalism are no more in line with the teaching of the Church than are those who go to the opposite erroneous extreme of making an idol of one's nation.

In line with this traditional teaching, the *Compendium of the Social Doctrine of the Church* affirms that, though nations must exclude "every abuse of basic human rights and in particular the oppression of minorities", at the same time

> a nation has a "fundamental right to existence," to "its own language and culture, through which a people expresses and promotes ... its fundamental spiritual 'sovereignty,'" to "shape its life according to its own traditions..." ... [and] to "build its future by providing an appropriate education for the younger generation." (157)

This right has implications for minority communities. In the encyclical *Pacem in Terris*, Pope Saint John XXIII insisted that nations treat minority ethnic communities justly, "especially in what concerns their language, culture, ancient traditions, and their economic activity and enterprise" (96). But he also cautioned that minority communities have an obligation to respect and to integrate into the culture of the larger nation within which they reside. He wrote:

> It is worth noting, however, that these minority groups, in reaction, perhaps, to the enforced hardships of their present situation, or to historical circumstances, frequently tend to magnify unduly characteristics proper to their own people. They even rate them above those human values which are common to all mankind, as though the good of the entire human family should subserve the interests of their own particular groups. A more reasonable attitude for such people to adopt would be to recognize the advantages, too, which accrue to them from their own special situation. They should realize that their constant association with a people steeped in a different civilization from their own has no small part to play in the development of their own particular genius and spirit. Little by little they can absorb into their very being those virtues which characterize the other nation. But for this to happen these minority groups must enter into some kind of association with the people

in whose midst they are living, and learn to share their customs and way of life. It will never happen if they sow seeds of disaffection which can only produce a harvest of evils, stifling the political development of nations. (97)

It is in light of these principles that we need to understand the issue of immigration. The *Catechism* teaches:

> The more prosperous nations are obliged, to the extent they are able, to welcome the *foreigner* in search of the security and the means of livelihood which he cannot find in his country of origin. Public authorities should see to it that the natural right is respected that places a guest under the protection of those who receive him.
>
> Political authorities, for the sake of the common good for which they are responsible, may make the exercise of the right to immigrate subject to various juridical conditions, especially with regard to the immigrants' duties toward their country of adoption. Immigrants are obliged to respect with gratitude the material and spiritual heritage of the country that receives them, to obey its laws and to assist in carrying civic burdens. (2241)

On the one hand, the *Catechism* says, a prosperous nation ought to welcome immigrants, especially those in need. This is a theme on which Pope Francis has put special emphasis. The Holy Father has urged nations to be open to "refugees fleeing from hunger, war and other grave dangers", noting:

In each of these people, forced to flee to safety, Jesus is present as he was at the time of Herod. In the faces of the hungry, the thirsty, the naked, the sick, strangers and prisoners, we are called to see the face of Christ who pleads with us to help.[9]

Calling attention to the variety of difficulties faced by immigrants, the pope notes that "particularly disturbing are those situations where migration is not only involuntary, but actually set in motion by various forms of human trafficking and enslavement."[10] Francis has also condemned the scapegoating of immigrants, lamenting:

Migrants, refugees, displaced persons and victims of trafficking have become emblems of exclusion. In addition to the hardships that their condition entails, they are often looked down upon and considered the source of all society's ills.[11]

The pope has urged that when taking in immigrants, "the family's integrity must always be promoted, supporting family reunifications—including grandparents, grandchildren and siblings."[12] He has repeatedly emphasized that a proper attitude toward

[9] Message of His Holiness Pope Francis for the 106th World Day of Migrants and Refugees (May 13, 2020).

[10] Message of His Holiness Pope Francis for the World Day of Migrants and Refugees (August 5, 2013).

[11] Message of His Holiness Pope Francis for the 105th World Day of Migrants and Refugees (April 30, 2019).

[12] Message of His Holiness Pope Francis for the 104th World Day of Migrants and Refugees (August 15, 2017).

immigrants "may be articulated by four verbs: to *welcome*, to *protect*, to *promote* and to *integrate*".[13]

On the other hand, the *Catechism* is clear that the duty to welcome immigrants does not entail that a nation has an obligation to take in all foreigners who want to enter, or that it must take foreigners in unconditionally. As previously stated, nations are obligated to welcome foreigners "*to the extent they are able*". Immigrants are obligated "to respect ... [the] *spiritual heritage*" of the nation they enter, "to *obey its laws* and to *assist in carrying civic burdens*". The *Catechism* is not advocating open borders, it is not teaching that nations must tolerate illegal immigration, and it is not ignoring the relevance of cultural considerations to immigration policy. Pope Francis, too, has affirmed that "those who arrive ... are duty bound not to close themselves off from the culture and traditions of the receiving country, respecting above all its laws."[14] And he has acknowledged:

> The presence of migrants and refugees seriously challenges the various societies which accept them. Those societies are faced with new situations which could create serious hardship unless they are suitably motivated, managed and regulated.[15]

---

[13] Address of His Holiness Pope Francis to Participants in the International Forum on "Migration and Peace" (February 21, 2017). The pope has reiterated these four themes in subsequent statements.

[14] Ibid.

[15] Message of His Holiness Pope Francis for the World Day of Migrants and Refugees (September 12, 2015).

Similarly, in 2001 Pope John Paul II acknowledged that even "highly developed countries are not always able to assimilate all those who emigrate", and that while the Church strongly affirms the right to emigrate, "certainly, the exercise of such a right is to be regulated, because practicing it indiscriminately may do harm and be detrimental to the common good of the community that receives the migrant."[16] In 1995, he emphasized the need to welcome migrants, to take account of the dangerous circumstances they are sometimes fleeing, and to avoid all racist and xenophobic attitudes. At the same time, he acknowledged that "migration is assuming the features of a social emergency, above all because of the increase in *illegal migrants*" (emphasis in the pope's own text), and that the problem is "delicate and complex".[17] He affirmed that "illegal immigration should be prevented" and that one reason it is problematic is that "the supply of foreign labour is becoming excessive in comparison to the needs of the economy, which already has difficulty in absorbing its domestic workers"; in some cases, it may be necessary to advise migrants "to seek acceptance in other countries, or to return to their own country".[18] As Pope Francis

[16] Message of the Holy Father for the 87th World Day of Migration (February 2, 2001), no. 3.

[17] *Undocumented Migrants* (Message of Pope John Paul II for World Migration Day) (July 25, 1995), nos. 1 and 5.

[18] Ibid., nos. 2 and 4.

has said, as nations work together to address the plight of migrants,

> it must also be emphasized that such cooperation begins with the efforts of each country to create better economic and social conditions at home, so that emigration will not be the only option left for those who seek peace, justice, security and full respect of their human dignity. The creation of opportunities for employment in the local economies will also avoid the separation of families and ensure that individuals and groups enjoy conditions of stability and serenity.[19]

Such considerations have nothing to do with hostility to or insensitivity toward migrants, but rather with the fact that when resources are limited, our first duty is to those to whom we have special attachments and obligations, in the case of our own countrymen just as in the case of our own families. As Saint Thomas Aquinas teaches:

> Augustine says ... "Since one cannot do good to all, we ought to consider those chiefly who by reason of place, time or any other circumstance, by a kind of chance are more closely united to us."...
>
> Now the order of nature is such that every natural agent pours forth its activity first and most of all on the things which are nearest to it.... But

[19] Message of His Holiness Pope Francis for the World Day of Migrants and Refugees (August 5, 2013).

the bestowal of benefits is an act of charity towards others. Therefore we ought to be most beneficent towards those who are most closely connected with us.

Now one man's connection with another may be measured in reference to the various matters in which men are engaged together; (thus the intercourse of kinsmen is in natural matters, that of fellow-citizens is in civic matters, that of the faithful is in spiritual matters, and so forth): and various benefits should be conferred in various ways according to these various connections, because we ought in preference to bestow on each one such benefits as pertain to the matter in which, speaking simply, he is most closely connected with us....

For it must be understood that, other things being equal, one ought to succor those rather who are most closely connected with us.[20]

Cultural considerations no less than economic ones are relevant to the imperative to tailor immigration policy in a way that preserves the well-being of one's nation, for a nation is not merely a population located in a certain geographical territory. It is, as Pope John Paul II emphasized, united by a common history, traditions, mores, language, et cetera, and disruptions to these cultural ties can therefore threaten its unity. It is for this reason that Saint Thomas taught that a state must take caution when

[20] *ST* II-II.31.3.

allowing large numbers of unassimilated foreigners
into its midst. In *On Kingship*, he argues that it can
be "harmful to civic customs" when trade results
in a large population of foreign nationals residing
continually in a country, "for it is inevitable that
strangers, brought up under other laws and customs, will in many cases act as the citizens are not
wont to act and thus, since the citizens are drawn
by their example to act likewise, their own civic
life is upset."[21] Similarly, of ancient Israel, Aquinas
observes approvingly in the *Summa Theologiae*:

> When any foreigners wished to be admitted
> entirely to their fellowship ... a certain order was
> observed. For they were not at once admitted to
> citizenship: just as it was law with some nations that
> no one was deemed a citizen except after two or
> three generations.... The reason for this was that if
> foreigners were allowed to meddle with the affairs
> of a nation as soon as they settled down in its midst,
> many dangers might occur, since the foreigners not
> yet having the common good firmly at heart might
> attempt something hurtful to the people.[22]

What these passages imply is that too free a flow
of populations across borders can dilute allegiance to
the shared norms and culture of a nation and thereby

[21] Thomas Aquinas, *On Kingship*, trans. Gerald B. Phelan (Toronto:
Pontifical Institute of Mediaeval Studies, 1949), 76.
[22] *ST* I-II.105.3.

threaten national unity. On the side of a nation's citizens, out of deference to foreigners, they might become less inclined to uphold their unifying norms and culture, and thus less attached to their own nation; on the side of foreigners, they might feel less incentive to adopt or respect the norms and culture themselves, and thus less likely to integrate into the extended family of the nation that adopts them.

A contemporary example of the first sort of phenomenon is the rise of what philosopher Roger Scruton calls "oikophobia", or repudiation of one's own nation, evident in Westerners who disdain patriotism and bitterly denounce their own countries and civilization as inherently and uniquely racist and oppressive.[23] (See the discussion of Critical Race Theory in the chapters to follow.) An example of the second sort of phenomenon would be the existence in European cities of immigrant enclaves or "ghettos" in which outsiders are unwelcome, Sharia law governs, and radicalism is fostered. Both sorts of phenomena can lead to a xenophobic backlash among citizens who worry that national unity is threatened. Aquinas' teaching implies that it is legitimate for public authorities to formulate immigration policy in a way that will mitigate such potential problems.

[23] Roger Scruton, *The Need for Nations* (London: Civitas, 2004), chap. 8.

Such examples, along with the statements about cultural integration from recent popes and the *Catechism* quoted above, show that these considerations remain as relevant to applying the Church's teaching today as they were in Saint Thomas' day. Indeed, as the 1988 document *The Church and Racism* acknowledges:

> It is up to the public powers who are responsible for the common good to determine the number of refugees or immigrants which their country can accept, taking into consideration its possibilities for employment and its perspectives for development but also the urgency of the need of other people. The State must also see to it that a serious social imbalance is not created which would be accompanied by sociological phenomena of rejection such as those which can occur when an overly heavy concentration of persons from another culture is perceived as directly threatening the identity and customs of the local community that receives them.[24]

Similarly, acknowledging concerns about potential cultural friction between immigrant communities and citizens of the countries that take them in, Pope Saint John Paul II noted that:

[24] Pontifical Commission on Justice and Peace, *The Church and Racism: Towards a More Fraternal Society* (Vatican City: Pontificia Commissio Iustitia et Pax, 1988), no. 29.

If the gradual integration of all immigrants is fostered with respect for their identity and, at the same time, safeguarding the cultural patrimony of the peoples who receive them, there is less of a risk that they will come together to form real "ghettos" in which they remain isolated from the social context and sometimes even end by harbouring a desire to take over the territory gradually.[25]

Pope Benedict XVI, too, acknowledged that host countries have a "legitimate concern for security and social coherence" so that "states have the right to regulate migration flows and to defend their own frontiers" and "immigrants, moreover, have the duty to integrate into the host country, respecting its laws and its national identity."[26] And Pope Francis, notwithstanding his special concern for migrants and refugees, has also said:

What do I think of countries that close their frontiers? I think that, in theory, hearts must not be closed to refugees, but those who govern need prudence. They must be very open to receiving refugees, but they also have to calculate how best to settle them, because refugees must not only be accepted, but also integrated.... [A] political price can be paid for an imprudent judgement, for

---

[25] Message of the Holy Father John Paul II for the 90th World Day of Migrants and Refugees (December 15, 2003), no. 5.

[26] Message of His Holiness Benedict XVI for the 97th World Day of Migrants and Refugees (September 27, 2010).

accepting more than can be integrated. What is
the danger when refugees or migrants—and this
applies to everybody—are not integrated? They
become a ghetto. A culture that does not develop
in relationship with another culture, this is dangerous.... I talked with an official of the Swedish
government ... [who] told me of some difficulties
they are presently facing ... because so many are
arriving that there is no time to make provision
for them, so that they can find schools, homes,
employment, and learn the language. Prudence has
to make this calculation.[27]

The economic and cultural considerations that
have been mentioned by the popes have nothing
whatsoever to do with race. Nor do they in any
way nullify the Church's teaching on the obligation to welcome and help the stranger. The point is
simply that the Church herself acknowledges that a
nation has a right to put conditions on immigration
in order to protect its own well-being. How best to
balance the needs of immigrants and the interests of
the receiving nation and its people can in some concrete circumstances be a difficult matter, on which
Catholics of good will can reasonably disagree. It is
therefore unjust, uncharitable, and contrary to the
Church's teaching peremptorily to dismiss all concerns about national identity and the economic and

[27] In-Flight Press Conference of His Holiness Pope Francis from
Sweden to Rome (November 1, 2016).

cultural consequences of immigration as motivated by racism or other forms of bigotry.

Of course, it is true that some might try to distort this aspect of the Church's teaching and make of it a rationalization for racism and xenophobia. But that is an argument for presenting the teaching accurately, not for ignoring it. To paraphrase G. K. Chesterton, to object to patriotic concerns about national identity on the grounds that they are sometimes used as a cover for hostility to foreigners is like objecting to romantic love on the grounds that it has sometimes led a jealous lover to murder a rival.[28] We should object strenuously to all abuse of a teaching, but always while upholding the teaching itself.

Moreover, the danger here is not all in one direction. True, we should never allow the Church's teaching on patriotism and the rights of a nation to protect its cultural identity to serve as an excuse for racism and xenophobia. But neither should we allow false accusations of racism and xenophobia to serve as an excuse for ignoring the Church's teaching on patriotism and the rights of a nation to protect its cultural identity.

Some Catholics might wonder whether the ship has at this point already left the harbor—whether the Church's traditional teaching on the nation is

---

[28] Cited in Scruton, *The Need for Nations*, 3. The particular abuse of patriotism that Chesterton himself had in mind was using it as an excuse for warmongering.

now out of date and ought to be abandoned, in view of the rise of multinational corporations and the global economy, the power of supranational institutions such as the World Trade Organization and the European Union, the prevalence of multiculturalist ideas and policies, and so on. But this is like saying that the Church's teaching on sexual morality is out of date and ought to be abandoned, in view of the prevalence of abortion, divorce, fornication, homosexuality, contraception, et cetera. The Church has a duty to present the *entirety* of her teaching, not merely those aspects of it that modern people are willing to follow or which are otherwise inoffensive to the secular conventional wisdom. Indeed, it is precisely the least popular aspects of her teaching which the secular world stands most in need of hearing.

Moreover, that the Church's traditional teaching on patriotism and the nation is in fact especially relevant today is demonstrated by the recent resurgence of populist and antiglobalist movements in Europe and the United States. As Pope John Paul II taught, the nation is a natural institution and a sense of national loyalty fulfills a natural human need. When that need is not met in a healthy way, people will try to satisfy it in unhealthy ways. And when governments ignore legitimate concerns about national identity and working class economic interests—indiscriminately dismissing all expressions of such concern as racist or otherwise bigoted—they thereby *increase* rather than decrease the likelihood of the sort of ugly xenophobic overreaction they are hoping to avoid. As Chesterton argued: "What we really need for the frustration and overthrow of a deaf and raucous Jingoism is a renascence of the love of the native land. When that comes, all shrill cries will cease suddenly."[29] The Church's teaching on patriotism and on the nation as a natural institution is in no way a concession to nationalism, racism, or xenophobia but precisely a *corrective* to them. It is the sober middle ground between these errors on the one hand, and the excessive individualism and globalism that tend to dissolve national loyalties on the other.

[29] G. K. Chesterton, "In Defence of Patriotism", in *The Defendant* (London: R. Brimley Johnson, 1901), 167.

4

What Is Critical Race Theory?

Another area where the Church's teaching provides a needed corrective concerns the rise of Critical Race Theory (often abbreviated CRT), which was first developed by academic legal theorists such as Derrick Bell, Alan Freeman, and Kimberlé Crenshaw, and has recently been popularized by the bestsellers Ibram X. Kendi's *How to Be an Antiracist* and Robin DiAngelo's *White Fragility*, among others.[1] Because CRT is energetically promoted in the name of "antiracism", many suppose that it must be benign. This is as naïve as thinking that Marxism

[1] Ibram X. Kendi, *How to Be an Antiracist* (New York: One World, 2019) and Robin DiAngelo, *White Fragility: Why It's So Hard for White People to Talk about Racism* (Boston: Beacon Press, 2018). For a general survey of the main ideas and academic literature, see Richard Delgado and Jean Stefancic, *Critical Race Theory: An Introduction*, 3rd ed. (New York: New York University Press, 2017). For a collection of articles by the movement's founding thinkers, see Kimberlé Crenshaw, Neil Gotanda, Gary Peller, and Kendall Thomas, eds., *Critical Race Theory: The Key Writings that Formed the Movement* (New York: The New Press, 1995).

must be benign given that it presents itself as an ally of the working class. In fact, Marxism has only ever yielded an oppression even worse than the kind it claims to eradicate. Similarly, in the name of remedying the evil of racism, CRT actually promotes a novel and insidious form of racism. Like Marxism, CRT is a grave perversion of the good cause it claims to represent, and it is utterly incompatible with Catholic social teaching.

Let us first survey the main claims of Critical Race Theory, and then consider the philosophical and social scientific objections against it, as well as the many ways CRT conflicts with the teaching of the Church. The fundamental assertion of CRT is that racism absolutely permeates the nooks and crannies of every social institution and the psyches of every individual. It goes especially deep in each individual white person, but it infects even the thinking of nonwhite people insofar as they have bought into the racist assumptions that whites have about them and acquiesced to the racist policies and institutions by which whites oppress them. Accordingly, a "system of white-over-color ascendency" is, claims CRT, "ordinary, not aberrational,... [and] the usual way society does business."[2] "No aspect of society", insists DiAngelo, "is outside of ... the forces of racism."[3] Nonwhite people suffocate under

---

[2] Delgado and Stefancic, *Critical Race Theory*, 8.
[3] DiAngelo, *White Fragility*, 13.

a regime of "racist power", "white privilege", and indeed "white supremacy".[4]

For readers unacquainted with CRT, such phrases might call to mind stereotypical examples of racist behavior and policy—Ku Klux Klan rallies and cross burnings, Jim Crow laws that enforced racial segregation in the American South, apartheid in South Africa, and so forth. Given that such policies have long been abolished in the United States and South Africa, and that the KKK and similar organizations are widely regarded as disreputable and have only marginal influence, talk of "white supremacy" and the like might seem overheated, to say the least. But this sort of thing is not what CRT writers have in mind when they use such language. They hold that even societies free of such overt expressions of bigotry, and even whites who explicitly reject racism, are in fact racist, usually without realizing it. Indeed, "racism ... pervades every vestige of our reality."[5]

How does this purportedly omnipresent racism manifest itself? CRT writers claim, first, that it is evident in any "inequity" or "disparity" that exists between whites and members of other racial groups. For example, suppose 10 percent of the

[4] Such expressions are peppered liberally throughout CRT literature, but see Delgado and Stefancic, *Critical Race Theory*, 85–92 and DiAngelo, *White Fragility*, chap. 2 for sustained expositions of how they are understood by CRT writers.

[5] DiAngelo, *White Fragility*, 72. DiAngelo is here quoting approvingly from Omowale Akintunde.

population of a certain country is black, but that blacks make up less than 10 percent of the doctors or stockbrokers in that country. This, allege CRT writers, is a manifestation of racism. Kendi takes the very existence of such "racial inequity" to be *the* hallmark of "racist policy", "systemic racism", "institutional racism", or "structural racism".[6] He peremptorily states: "As an anti-racist, when I see racial disparities, I see racism."[7] DiAngelo holds that "attributing inequality between whites and people of color to causes other than racism"—for example, suggesting that differences in racial representation in such professions reflect cultural differences between racial or ethnic groups—is itself to "enact racism".[8] "To be antiracist", Kendi says, "is to view the inequities between all racialized ethnic groups as a problem of *policy*" rather than cultural values, behavior, or any other factor.[9] It is to hold that only "policies determine the success of groups" and that "it is racist power that creates the policies that cause racial inequities."[10]

[6] Kendi, *How to Be an Antiracist*, 18.

[7] Quoted in " 'When I See Racial Disparities, I See Racism': Discussing Race, Gender and Mobility", *New York Times*, March 27, 2018, https://www.nytimes.com/interactive/2018/03/27/upshot/reader-questions-about-race-gender-and-mobility.html.

[8] DiAngelo, *White Fragility*, 43–44.

[9] Kendi, *How to Be an Antiracist*, 64. Emphasis added.

[10] Ibid., 94.

According to Critical Race Theorists, racism also manifests itself through "micro-aggressions" and "implicit bias". "Micro-aggressions" are characterized by one influential introduction to CRT as "small acts of racism, consciously or unconsciously perpetrated, welling up from the assumptions about racial matters most of us absorb from the cultural heritage in which we come of age" in a country like the United States.[11] The examples given include a white cashier who fails to smile or make small talk with a nonwhite customer and a white pedestrian who fails to return the acknowledgement of a passing nonwhite jogger. Alleged racism of this sort is so subtle that it is "usually unnoticed by members of the majority race".[12] All the same, Kendi objects to calling such acts "micro-aggressions" on the grounds that the term is too mild. They are, he says, more accurately described as acts of "racist abuse".[13]

"Implicit bias" is defined as "unconscious association of one idea with another, such as race and personal qualities, frequently evincing a negative attitude."[14] For example, it might involve "unintentionally discriminating against people of color during [a] hiring process" or "anti-black feelings that ... can and do seep out without [one's] awareness"

[11] Delgado and Stefancic, *Critical Race Theory*, 2.
[12] Ibid., 179.
[13] Kendi, *How to Be an Antiracist*, 47.
[14] Delgado and Stefancic, *Critical Race Theory*, 176.

when, for example, passing a black person on the
street.[15] Here too the purported racism is so subtle
that only when, via CRT, "our antiracist eyes are
open to seeing" it can we do so.[16] Indeed, it exists
even in those who are self-consciously opposed
to racism and unconcerned with skin color. Di-
Angelo warns of "a manifestation of racism that
well-intentioned people who see themselves as educated and progressive are more likely to exhibit"
because it "exists under the surface of consciousness ... [and] conflicts with consciously held beliefs
of racial equality and justice".[17] Racism thus lurks
unconsciously even in those who by all conventional standards would be paradigmatic examples of
nonracists. "The language of color blindness—like
the language of 'not racist' – is", Kendi says, in reality, "a mask to hide racism."[18]

In the view of these CRT writers, those who
deny harboring racism only confirm that they are
racists precisely by denying it. DiAngelo assigns
the label "white fragility" to the tendency of white
people to take offense at the accusation that they
are racist. In her view, "the defensiveness that
ensues upon any suggestion of racial bias ... is clas-
sic white fragility because it protects our racial bias

[15] DiAngelo, *White Fragility*, 42 and 90.
[16] Kendi, *How to Be an Antiracist*, 221.
[17] DiAngelo, *White Fragility*, 43.
[18] Kendi, *How to Be an Antiracist*, 10.

while simultaneously affirming our identities as open-minded."[19] White fragility is manifest in those who respond to the accusation that they are racist with "argumentation" and other forms of disagreement.[20] Its function is to serve as "a powerful means of white racial control and the protection of white advantage".[21] Indeed, to dare to take offense at or to disagree with the CRT analysis is itself a form of "bullying".[22] The reality, DiAngelo says, is that whites who are told they are racist are merely being "educated" and made "more racially aware", and the response they should be giving to the CRT thinkers and activists who provide this education is to say, "Thank you."[23] "The heartbeat of racism is denial", says Kendi, and "the heartbeat of antiracism is confession."[24]

The malign source of this "systemic racism", say CRT writers, is "whiteness", a "quality pertaining to Euro-American or Caucasian people or traditions".[25] Hence a subfield within CRT known as Critical White Studies is devoted to "the study of the white race" and of "white consciousness" and the "white privilege" and "white solidarity" by which

---

[19] DiAngelo, *White Fragility*, 42.
[20] Ibid., 2 and 101.
[21] Ibid., 2.
[22] Ibid., 112.
[23] Ibid., 125 and 150.
[24] Kendi, *How to Be an Antiracist*, 235.
[25] Delgado and Stefancic, *Critical Race Theory*, 186.

"white supremacy" is maintained.[26] Once again, the
unwary reader might suppose the reference here to
be to the KKK, neo-Nazi skinheads, segregationists, and other such marginal persons, and might be
baffled that anyone could take such racists to have
much power or influence today. But again, what
CRT writers are talking about is not these sorts
of people, but rather a purported racism that is so
subtle that it permeates even the thinking of those
who regard themselves as progressive and opposed
to racism. And CRT regards this subtle racism as an
iceberg of which the outright forms of racism of the
past were but the tip; thus the elimination of segregation and the like has done little to improve things.
Bell argues that integration and related policies were
enacted only insofar as they benefited whites.[27] One
prominent mainstream academic book on CRT
floats the proposal that "white privilege" is still so
pervasive a feature of American society that even
in the absence of "outright racism ... our system
of white over black/brown ... remain[s] virtually
unchanged ... so that we remain roughly as we were
before."[28] Indeed, DiAngelo claims that the subtle
forms of racism CRT claims to identify "in some

[26] Ibid., 85f.

[27] See Derrick A. Bell, Jr., "*Brown v. Board of Education* and the
Interest Convergence Dilemma", in Crenshaw, et al., eds., *Critical
Race Theory*, 22–23.

[28] Delgado and Stefancic, *Critical Race Theory*, 90–91.

ways ... are more sinister than concrete rules such as Jim Crow".[29] Nor is it the United States alone that is governed by "white supremacy". According to DiAngelo, by way of American economic, cultural, and military power, "white supremacy is circulated globally [and] this powerful ideology promotes the idea of whiteness as the ideal for humanity well beyond the West."[30]

"Whiteness", claims DiAngelo, is so thoroughly malign that "anti-blackness is foundational to our very identities as white people."[31] Hence, while a sense of racial identity and solidarity can be a healthy thing for nonwhites, in DiAngelo's view "a positive white identity is an impossible goal" for "white identity is inherently racist [and] white people do not exist outside the system of white supremacy."[32] It is therefore incumbent on whites to "struggle with ... [their] white fragility" and "strive to be 'less white'" by facing up to their racism and abandoning their privilege.[33] Since their racism is so subtle and runs so deep, this is a "lifelong work that is uniquely [theirs]", and since their "learning will never be finished, neither will the need to hold [them] accountable."[34]

[29] DiAngelo, *White Fragility*, 50.
[30] Ibid., 29.
[31] Ibid., 91.
[32] Ibid., 149.
[33] Ibid., 150.
[34] Ibid., 33 and 152.

Whites need to become accustomed to "discomfort", to feeling "unmoored" and "not knowing" so as to achieve "racial humility".[35] "[They] need to feel grief about the brutality of white supremacy and [their] role in it."[36] In the light of CRT analysis, another influential work concludes, "No white member of society seems quite so innocent."[37]

It might seem obviously absurd to attribute guilt to any particular white person in the absence of evidence that he intentionally acted to cause harm to nonwhite people or that he is otherwise at fault for racial disparities. But CRT theorists like Freeman claim that the very idea that we should look at the issue in terms of specific actions or persons who might be identified as "causes" or at "fault" reflects the "perpetrator perspective", and that we ought instead to adopt a "victim perspective" that focuses simply on the condition of minority groups that are disadvantaged rather than on its cause.[38] Crenshaw insists on characterizing misfortunes suffered by minorities as "patterns of subordination", whether or not they were "intentionally produced".[39]

[35] Ibid., 14.

[36] Ibid., 137.

[37] Delgado and Stefancic, Critical Race Theory, 91.

[38] Alan David Freeman, "Legitimizing Racial Discrimination through Antidiscrimination Law: A Critical Review of Supreme Court Doctrine", in Crenshaw, et al., eds., Critical Race Theory, 30.

[39] Kimberlé Williams Crenshaw, "Mapping the Margins: Intersectionality, Identity Politics, and Violence against Women of Color", in Crenshaw, et al., eds., Critical Race Theory, 359.

What does combatting "whiteness" and "systemic racism" entail at the level of public policy? CRT advocates hold that "only aggressive, color-conscious efforts" on behalf of nonwhite people will do the job.[40] This will require racial discrimination in their favor and against whites. Bell insists that policies like racial equality and applying the same abstract legal principles to everyone actually favors whites.[41] Accordingly, one CRT thinker proposes that "admissions officers discount, or penalize, the scores of [white, suburban] candidates" because of their "white privilege".[42] Some CRT activists even debate whether "whites [should] be welcome in the movement and at its workshops and conferences".[43] Kendi holds that "racial discrimination is not inherently racist" and that, indeed, "if discrimination is creating equity, then it is antiracist."[44] He continues:

> The only remedy to racist discrimination is antiracist discrimination. The only remedy to past discrimination is present discrimination. The only remedy to present discrimination is future discrimination.[45]

[40] Delgado and Stefancic, *Critical Race Theory*, 27.

[41] Derrick A. Bell, Jr., "Racial Realism", in Crenshaw et al., eds., *Critical Race Theory*, 304 and 307.

[42] Delgado and Stefancic report this proposal matter-of-factly, *Critical Race Theory*, 134.

[43] Ibid., 105.

[44] Kendi, *How to Be an Antiracist*, 19.

[45] Ibid.

Moreover, such discrimination must continue into the future as long as any racial inequities exist, no matter how ineffective particular policies may be in eliminating them. "When policies fail ... start over and seek out new and more effective antiracist treatments until they work."[46]

For some CRT writers, "campus speech codes" and "tort remedies for racist speech" may also be required.[47] Some advocate "criminalization" of such speech, and others "a new independent tort in which the victims of deliberate, face-to-face vituperation could sue and prove damages".[48] Given how broadly CRT writers define terms such as "racism" and "aggression", such policing of speech is bound to be extensive. "Economic boycotts" will be also necessary, and indeed, antiracist transformation may have to be "convulsive and cataclysmic" rather than involving a "peaceful transition".[49] If so, then "critical theorists and activists will need to provide criminal defense for resistance movements and activists and to articulate theories and strategies for that resistance."[50]

Readers unfamiliar with Critical Race Theory might be shocked by such extremism. They may be

---

[46] Ibid., 232.
[47] Delgado and Stefancic, *Critical Race Theory*, 25.
[48] Ibid., 125.
[49] Ibid., 154–55.
[50] Ibid.

used to associating opposition to racism with liberalism, which, traditionally, insists on respecting rights to free speech, nondiscrimination, judging people as individuals rather than on the basis of group membership, and rational persuasion and legal reform rather than coercion. However, CRT is like Marxism in regarding liberalism as insufficiently radical and, indeed, as reactionary. CRT rejects "traditional civil rights discourse, which stresses incrementalism and step-by-step progress", and instead "questions the very foundations of the liberal order", including ideas such as "Enlightenment rationalism", "neutral principles of constitutional law", "color blindness", "equal treatment for all persons", and "rights".[51] Bell holds that such notions actually harm blacks.[52] DiAngelo dismisses "individualism and color blindness" as "ideologies of racism", and "objectivity" along with them.[53] "Contrary to the ideology of individualism," she says, "we represent our groups and those who have come before us", and "we don't see through clear or objective eyes—we see through racial lenses."[54] Crenshaw suggests that it is politically inexpedient for black people to think of themselves primarily as *persons* (as opposed to primarily as *black* persons,

[51] Ibid., 4, 26, and 28–29.
[52] Bell, "Racial Realism", 304 and 306–7.
[53] DiAngelo, *White Fragility*, 9 and 89.
[54] Ibid., 85–86.

specifically).[55] Kendi regards the push for a "race-neutral" society to be in fact "the most threatening racist movement".[56] He, too, holds that "objectivity [is] really 'collective subjectivity'" and that "it is impossible to be objective."[57] Happily embracing the relativism such views entail, he maintains that "cultural relativity [is] the essence of cultural antiracism."[58]

If there are no neutral, objective, rational standards by reference to which Critical Race Theorists and those who disagree with them can settle their disputes, what is left? How might hearts and minds be changed? Kendi does not shrink from drawing the obvious conclusion. "The problem of race", he says, "has always been at its core the problem of power, not the problem of immorality or ignorance."[59] The question of how to change hearts and minds is therefore not to the point. What matters is power. He continues:

> The original problem of racism has not been solved by suasion. Knowledge is only power if knowledge is put to the struggle for power. Changing minds is not a movement... Changing minds is not

[55] Crenshaw, "Mapping the Margins", 375.

[56] Kendi, *How to Be an Antiracist*, 20.

[57] Ibid., 167. Kendi is here citing approvingly views he attributes to Molefi Kete Asante and Ama Mazama.

[58] Ibid., 91.

[59] Ibid., 208.

activism. An activist produces power and policy change, not mental change.[60]

Accordingly, Kendi advocates a movement in which "antiracists [are] propelled only by the craving for power to shape policy."[61]

Racism is not the only thing CRT writers think so permeates society that it must be ruthlessly extirpated. According to the CRT notion of "intersectionality", first introduced by Crenshaw, given the existence of categories such as "race, sex, class, national origin, and sexual orientation", many individuals "experience multiple forms of oppression".[62] Hence, the CRT analysis of racism is extended to analyses of "sexism", "classism", "homophobia", "transphobia", and so on. "Inequities", "micro-aggressions", "implicit bias", et cetera are to be ferreted out and combated in *all* of these cases. Hence, Kendi tells us that "capitalism is essentially racist; racism is essentially capitalist" and they "are two sides of the same destructive body", which "shall one day die together".[63] He says that "inequities between women and men" reflect "sexist policy" and that these too must be eliminated in the name of antiracism since "to truly be antiracist

---

[60] Ibid., 209.
[61] Ibid., 214.
[62] Delgado and Stefancic, *Critical Race Theory*, 58–59.
[63] Kendi, *How to Be an Antiracist*, 163.

is to be feminist".[64] Similarly, he says, "we cannot
be antiracist if we are homophobic or transphobic"
and thus must regard "religious-freedom laws ... as
taking away the rights of queer people".[65] In short,
"intersectional theory now gives all of humanity the
ability to understand the intersectional oppression
of their identities."[66]

The implications couldn't be more radical. Modern history, Kendi assures us, has been nothing other
than "a battle between racists and antiracists",[67] and
our current situation remains so: "Our world is suffering from metastatic cancer. Stage 4. Racism has
spread to nearly every part of the body politic."[68]
Even the extreme political measures described so
far will not be sufficient to remedy this. The human
soul itself must be transformed, for "like fighting
an addiction, being an antiracist requires persistent
self-awareness, constant self-criticism, and regular
self-examination ... a radical reorientation of our
consciousness."[69] Neutrality in the struggle must
not be permitted. One cannot claim to be nonrac-
ist while refraining from endorsing CRT analysis
and policy. "One either allows racial inequities to

[64] Ibid., 189.
[65] Ibid., 197.
[66] Ibid., 191.
[67] Ibid., 150.
[68] Ibid., 234.
[69] Ibid., 23.

persevere, as a racist, or confronts racial inequities, as an antiracist", insists Kendi. "There is no in-between safe space of 'not racist.' The claim of 'not racist' neutrality is a mask for racism."[70] In short, anyone who dissents from CRT is to be regarded as among the ranks of the racist enemy.

[70] Ibid., 9.

5

Philosophical Problems with Critical Race Theory

I have quoted from mainstream and best-selling works of Critical Race Theory as well as from the academic theorists who influenced them, and I have done so at length, so that the reader can see just how extreme these increasingly popular views really are. Readers familiar with Marxism and postmodernism will have noted the similarities CRT bears to them, the main difference being that CRT substitutes an obsession with race for the Marxist's obsession with class and speaks of "whiteness" rather than the bourgeoisie as the sinister power lurking behind all legal and cultural institutions. This is no accident, for Marxists and postmodernists such as Antonio Gramsci and Michel Foucault, respectively, were key influences on the development of CRT.[1]

[1] Richard Delgado and Jean Stefancic, *Critical Race Theory: An Introduction*, 3rd ed. (New York: New York University Press, 2017), 5. For a useful discussion of the philosophical influences on Critical

Indeed, it is no exaggeration to say that CRT is essentially a reformulation of some of the main themes of Marxism and postmodernism in racial terms. Where Marxism speaks of the conflict under capitalism between the oppressive bourgeoisie and the oppressed proletariat, CRT speaks of the struggle under "systemic racism" between an oppressive "whiteness" and oppressed "people of color". Where the postmodernist takes all norms and truth claims to be culturally relative and masks for the vested interests of power, CRT identifies this power in the case of European and American civilization with "white supremacy", specifically. Foucault's theory that malign power operates in "capillary" fashion, seeping down into every nook and cranny of the social order and the individual psyche, is applied by CRT to an analysis of the purported workings of "racist power". His critique of the imprisonment and the punishment of criminals as a mask for the

Race Theory, see Helen Pluckrose and James Lindsay, *Cynical Theories: How Activist Scholarship Made Everything about Race, Gender, and Identity—and Why This Harms Everybody* (Durham, N.C.: Pitchstone Publishing, 2020). As Pluckrose and Lindsay rightly note, the relationship between Marxism, postmodernism, and Critical Race Theory is complex, and there are important differences between these systems of thought (for example, Marxism was itself one of the "metanarratives" that postmodernists aimed to subvert). All the same, both postmodernist and Marxist ideas had a profound effect on Critical Race Theory (albeit in an altered form), as CRT writers like Delgado and Stefancic themselves acknowledge.

vested interests of bourgeois power is transformed by CRT into a critique of the American justice system as inherently racist, a tool by which the forces of white supremacy keep nonwhites in line. Gramsci's theory that bourgeois power maintains itself via "hegemony" over the institutions of civil society (law, education, media, etc.) is applied by CRT to an analysis of how all such institutions reflect the interests of "white supremacy". His strategy of replacing the hegemony of the bourgeoisie with a hegemony of Marxist intellectuals who would gradually take over the institutions in question is echoed by the way that CRT is currently working its way through American society via "antiracist" policies imposed by government agencies, college administrators, corporate personnel departments, and the like, which are applauded in mainstream news media, popular entertainment, and best-selling books. The insistence that all resistance to CRT stems from unconscious racism that must be ferreted out and confessed to is reminiscent of the "struggle sessions" by which Maoists in communist China sought to extirpate all "counterrevolutionary" thinking. The Marxist conceit that anyone who opposes communism must be a fascist is echoed in the insistence that anyone who opposes CRT must be a racist. The socialist tendency to regard all inequalities in wealth and power as intrinsically unjust is echoed in CRT insistence that "inequities" are necessarily the result of racism, sexism, homophobia, et cetera. And so on.

Like postmodernism and Marxism, Critical Race Theory is at bottom a philosophical position, even if it also makes claims of a social scientific nature. Yet one of the most striking things about the work of CRT writers is the extremely poor quality of its argumentation and analysis. Because these writers typically present their ideas with a matter-of-fact and even aggressive confidence, unsophisticated readers are liable to be unduly impressed. The self-assured style of this writing functions, whether by design or not, as a rhetorical device by which its intellectual flimsiness might be masked.

The first thing the philosophically sophisticated reader notices in the argumentation of Critical Race Theorists is its relentless, indeed shameless, commission of a variety of textbook logical fallacies.[2] Consider, for example, DiAngelo's allegation that attributing racial inequalities to causes other than racism is itself racist, and her dismissal of all

[2] Among the critics of CRT who develop this point is Jonathan D. Church, in *Reinventing Racism: Why "White Fragility" Is the Wrong Way to Think about Racial Inequality* (Lanham: Rowman and Littlefield, 2021), chap. 7. Treatments of the logical fallacies can be found in many textbooks of logic and critical thinking. Book-length treatments can be found in S. Morris Engel, *With Good Reason: An Introduction to Informal Fallacies*, 3rd ed. (New York: St. Martin's Press, 1986), and Douglas Walton, *Informal Logic: A Pragmatic Approach*, 2nd ed. (Cambridge: Cambridge University Press, 2008).

disagreement with her analysis as an expression of "white fragility", which functions to uphold "white advantage".[3] Allegations of this sort are routine in the rhetoric of CRT. For instance, Kendi asserts that to attribute group differences in economic outcomes to cultural differences, or to judge one group's cultural practices to be in some way inferior to those of another, is racist.[4]

The problem with remarks like these is that it is simply a matter of elementary logic that the truth of a claim, and the cogency of an argument, stand or fall completely independently of the character or interests of the person making it, its historical or cultural origins, the context in which it is made, and any other such considerations. To ignore this is to be guilty of a *fallacy of relevance*—the favorite such fallacy of CRT writers being the *ad hominem* fallacy, which itself comes in various forms. There is, for example, the *circumstantial ad hominem*, which involves rejecting a claim or argument simply because of some alleged vested interest on the part of the person advocating it. Suppose a greengrocer says that eating lots of fruits and vegetables is much healthier than eating lots of candy, and cites medical evidence to that effect. Would pointing out that he would benefit from

[3] Robin DiAngelo, *White Fragility: Why It's So Hard for White People to Talk about Racism* (Boston: Beacon Press, 2018), 2.
[4] Ibram X. Kendi, *How to Be an Antiracist* (New York: One World, 2019), 90 and 153–54.

people buying fruits and vegetables by itself give us sufficient reason to reject his claim or the evidence he cites? Of course not. A claim can still be true and the evidence for it strong whether or not the person making it would benefit in some way from its being true. Similarly, if a white person offers social scientific evidence for the claim that economic disparities between the races have more to do with factors such as fatherlessness and education than with racism, it is irrelevant to allege in response that such a claim would somehow uphold "white advantage". The claim that fatherlessness and education have a larger effect on economic outcomes than racism does could still be true, and the evidence for it might be strong, regardless of who may or may not benefit from its being true.

A related *ad hominem* fallacy is known in logic as *poisoning the well*. This involves trying to get people to ignore whatever some person says by casting aspersions on his character. For example, suppose you offer evidence that a change in tax policy might lead to economic growth. And suppose that, in response, your critics claim that you are mentally unbalanced, an alcoholic, or a serial adulterer and persuaded people to pay you no attention for these reasons. Of course, if these charges are false, they would be doing you a grave injustice. But the more important point for our purposes is that they would be completely irrelevant *even if they were true*. The claim that a change in tax policy would promote economic growth might be true and the arguments for it might be strong whether or not the person making the claim or giving the arguments is mentally unbalanced, an alcoholic, or an adulterer. In the same way, the objections raised against CRT by its critics might be good objections even if they were motivated by what DiAngelo calls "white fragility". When DiAngelo dismisses all criticism by attributing it to this purported psychological condition, she is committing a textbook example of the fallacy of poisoning the well.

Yet another common fallacy of relevance is known as the *genetic fallacy*, which involves rejecting a claim or an argument merely because of some disreputable historical or cultural associations it has or is alleged to have. For example, suppose someone dismissed all the evidence that smoking causes lung cancer on the grounds that some of the earliest research on the bad effects of tobacco use were carried out by scientists in Nazi Germany. Obviously this is a silly reason to reject the evidence in question. A claim might be true and the evidence for it strong even if some evil people happen to have believed it. Now, suppose a CRT writer dismisses the claim that some economic disparities between racial groups reflect cultural differences rather than racism, on the grounds that segregationists of the past also appealed to cultural differences to explain such economic disparities. This too would be a genetic fallacy. That immoral people like segregationists believed the claim that cultural differences can cause economic disparities doesn't entail that the claim is false, and it doesn't entail that anyone who believes that claim is morally on a par with segregationists.

The crudest form of the *ad hominem* fallacy is the *abusive ad hominem*, which involves the attempt to discredit what someone says merely by calling him names or otherwise insulting him. For example, suppose a politician argues for increasing vehicle taxes in order to fund highway repairs, and a rival responds by repeatedly labeling him a "communist" so as to stir up public hostility against him. He might thereby persuade people not to support the policy in question, but logically speaking, he has done absolutely nothing to show that the policy is not, in fact, a good one. Similarly, freely flinging the label "racist" at critics is a routine rhetorical tactic of CRT writers. Kendi's book *How to Be an Antiracist*, for instance, is largely page after page of undefended assertions to the effect that ideas and people Kendi doesn't like are "racist".

The general problem with *ad hominem* fallacies, and the reason they are classified as fallacies of relevance, is that they simply change the subject. What ultimately matters is whether a claim is true and whether the arguments for it are cogent. *Ad hominem* fallacies involve a failure to address those questions and instead focus on irrelevant matters such as the alleged character traits or motives of the people making a claim, the cultural baggage associated with it, and so on. Critical Race Theorists systematically commit such fallacies insofar as they routinely dismiss objections and lines of argument by labeling them "racist", alleging that they reflect "white fragility", and so on.

Another group of fallacies common in the rhetoric of CRT are *fallacies of presumption*. One such fallacy is known as *begging the question* (or *circular reasoning*), which involves arguing for a claim in a way that simply *presupposes* the claim, rather than offering any independent reason for believing it. For example, suppose I reason that Lucy would never lie to me because she loves me, and that I can know that she loves me because she told me so and would never lie to me. Obviously, I am arguing in a circle. I'm using the claim that she loves me as evidence that she wouldn't lie to me, while using the claim that she wouldn't lie to me as evidence that she loves me. I thus haven't given any real evidence for either of these claims at all, any more than I can pull myself up by my own bootstraps. Critical Race Theorists commit a similar fallacy when they support CRT by appealing to premises that nobody would accept who wasn't already committed to CRT.

DiAngelo essentially admits this when she writes that "Whiteness Studies begin with the premise that racism and white privilege exist in both traditional and modern forms, and rather than work to prove its existence, work to reveal it."[5] When such writers appeal, for example, to inequities, "microaggressions", and so on as evidence that "systemic racism" and "white privilege" are real, they are arguing in a circle, because nobody who didn't already believe that "systemic racism" and "white privilege" are real would consider these things evidence. In particular, nobody who doesn't already look at the world through CRT lenses would agree that the fact that blacks and Hispanics are underrepresented in STEM fields *by itself* demonstrates that there is racist discrimination in these fields against blacks and Hispanics, any more than the fact that Asians are overrepresented in STEM fields demonstrates that there is racist discrimination in favor of Asians. People who are not already committed to CRT would consider other explanations, such as cultural differences between racial and ethnic groups. Similarly, no one who does not already look at the world through CRT lenses would interpret every statement or action that a member of a minority group might find offensive as a racist "microaggression".

[5] Robin DiAngelo, "White Fragility", *International Journal of Critical Pedagogy* 3 (2018): 56.

Critical Race Theorists read evidence of racism *out of* such inequities, offenses, et cetera only because they first read racism *into* them. They are simply begging the question.

Another fallacy of presumption that goes to the very heart of Critical Race Theory is the fallacy of *special pleading*, which involves applying an arbitrary or unjustified double standard. Suppose, for example, that when criticizing a politician I disliked, I argued that no one who, like this particular politician, has been unfaithful to his wife should ever be trusted with public office. But suppose also that I favored electing some other adulterer and justified this by saying that since *he* had the right policies, his unfaithfulness could be overlooked. Obviously, I would be guilty of inconsistency. To be consistent, I would either have to stick to my initial claim that adulterers should never hold office, and therefore stop supporting the second candidate; or, if I insisted on continuing to support the second candidate, give up the objection I initially directed at the first candidate. What I cannot reasonably do is assert a general principle to which I make an arbitrary exception simply because it serves my interests to do so.

Critical Race Theory rests on several instances of the fallacy of special pleading. For example, under the influence of postmodernists like Foucault and Marxists like Gramsci, CRT writers routinely apply a "hermeneutics of suspicion" by which they claim to unmask all institutions, cultural assumptions, philosophical positions, and so on as nothing more than the instruments by which groups maintain power. What is distinctive of their analysis is an emphasis on *race* (rather than class, say) as definitive of these groups. Objectivity and race-neutrality are illusions, claim CRT writers. What we see as true or good reflects the racial lenses through which we look at the world rather than the world itself.

The trouble is that if Critical Race Theorists followed this out consistently, then they would have to acknowledge that *CRT itself* does not reflect objective reality, but merely the perspective and interests of CRT writers and those they claim to speak for. Critical Race Theorists would claim that their position is different from others insofar as, unlike the institutions and ideas that uphold "systemic racism" and "white supremacy", it does not reflect the interests of the powerful. But why should we believe that? After all, Friedrich Nietzsche, one of the fathers of the "hermeneutics of suspicion" and the source of Foucault's ideas, argued that *all* systems of thought reflect nothing more than the "will to power" of those who uphold them, including those that claim to favor the powerless. In particular, Nietzsche held that egalitarian moral and political doctrines such as socialism are nothing more than instruments by which the weak attempt to turn the tables on the strong—whom they know to be superior, and whom they envy and resent—and thereby to get revenge over them. Such doctrines have no more objective validity than nonegalitarian views do. Why not say the same of Critical Race Theory itself? Why not regard it too as merely another mask for the "will to power", worn by those who envy and resent whites—and thus as having no more objective validity or claim to truth than the views CRT criticizes?

The point is not to endorse Nietzsche's analysis, but rather to note that the "hermeneutics of suspicion" sword cuts both ways and inevitably skewers the person who wields it no less than his target. Some CRT writers, such as Crenshaw, see the problem and thus caution against embracing a thoroughgoing postmodernist relativism. But she has no principled reason for doing so, merely suggesting that it is "politically more empowering" to hold that at least some descriptions of social phenomena are objectively true, when doing so would favor the CRT analysis.[6] In fact, this does not solve the problem at all but instead exacerbates it, because she thereby implicitly admits that it is precisely a concern for power rather than for objective truth that motivates her position.

[6] Kimberlé Williams Crenshaw, "Mapping the Margins: Intersectionality, Identity Politics, and Violence against Women of Color", in Crenshaw et al., eds., *Critical Race Theory: The Key Writings That Formed the Movement* (New York: The New Press, 1996), 376.

Critical Race Theorists cannot logically have it both ways. If they insist that *all* systems of thought reflect only the interests of racial groups and have no objective validity, then this would undermine their own position no less than any other. If instead they acknowledge that it is possible to get beyond the perspective of one's own racial group and arrive at objective truth, then this would be the case for critics of CRT no less than for CRT writers—in which case CRT writers cannot dismiss rival views merely on the grounds that they purportedly reflect only the perspective of whites rather than objective reality.

Another way Critical Race Theorists commit the fallacy of special pleading concerns their interpretation of racial disparities. Consider the fact that "blacks are 13 percent of [the U.S.] population but 80 percent of professional basketball players and 65 percent of professional football players and among the highest-paid players in both sports."[7] Consider the fact that "Asians are overrepresented across all STEM occupational groups with higher than average shares among computer workers and life scientists, accounting for 19% of workers in both of these fields, which is much higher than their share in the

---

[7] Walter E. Williams, "Do Statistical Disparities Mean Injustice?", *Investor's Business Daily*, September 24, 2014, https://www.investors.com/politics/commentary/sometimes-our-differences-dont-indicate-victimhood/.

workforce overall (6%)."[8] Consider the fact that in the United States, "males are over-represented in prisons and jails" insofar as, despite their being just under half of the population, "ninety-two percent of people incarcerated in federal and state prisons are men."[9] Do the first two of these "inequities" entail that there exists racist discrimination against nonblacks and non-Asians? Does the third entail that there exists sexist discrimination against men? Of course not, and no one draws such conclusions. But those are the conclusions one would have to draw if one consistently applied CRT's "inequity" criterion of injustice; for if whites are overrepresented in some field, CRT writers insist that this *must* be due to racist discrimination or some related form of systemic injustice. Again, they cannot have it both ways. If they are to insist that disparities necessarily entail injustice in the one case, then they will have to conclude that they entail injustice in the others. If, more reasonably, they acknowledge that disparities are not always the result of racial discrimination or other injustice, then they will have to give up the claim that the underrepresentation of

[8] Cary Funk and Kim Parker, *Women and Men in STEM Often at Odds Over Workplace Equity*, Pew Research Center Report (January 9, 2018), 35.

[9] Rose Heyer and Peter Wagner, "Too Big to Ignore: How Counting People in Prisons Distorted Census 2000", *Prison Policy Initiative*, April 2004, https://www.prisonersofthecensus.org/toobig/.

blacks and Hispanics in some field, or the overrepresentation of whites in a field, necessarily entails
"systemic racism" or the like.

A third case of special pleading has to do with
generalizations about racial groups and their behaviors and cultural practices. As we've seen, if someone suggests that economic disparities between races
can be explained in part by cultural and behavioral
differences, such as the higher value put on education within some racial groups and higher rates of
fatherlessness within others, then writers like Di-
Angelo and Kendi will dismiss this as racist. "When
we racialize any group and then render that group's
culture inferior," Kendi says, "we are articulating
cultural racism."[10] Yet that is precisely what CRT
writers do when they make negative general characterizations about *whites* and *their* culture—to the
effect that there is such a thing as "white consciousness", that it is defined by "anti-blackness", that
"white identity is inherently racist", that "white fragility" is a defense mechanism to which all whites
are prone, and so on (to cite examples given earlier). Yet again, CRT writers illogically try to have
it both ways. But if they were consistent, then they
would either have to give up their negative general
characterizations of white culture; or, if they insist
that some negative general characterizations of white

[10] Kendi, *How to Be an Antiracist*, 90; cf. 153.

culture are true, then they would have to allow that some negative general characterizations of the cultures of other racial groups could be true too.

There are yet other elementary logical fallacies that are central to the argumentation of Critical Race Theorists. Consider the *fallacy of hypostatization*, which involves speaking of an abstraction as if it were a concrete reality. Suppose I complained that the economic system unjustly rewards people who write popular crime novels and unjustly punishes people like me, who write academic philosophy books that don't sell nearly as well. That makes it sound as if there were some concrete entity, "the economic system", that somehow works to ensure that things come out this way and can therefore be blamed for it. But of course, that's not the case. The reality is that there are simply many more people who enjoy crime novels than there are people who want to read philosophy books, and the lower earnings of writers of the latter are a consequence of that. Treating abstractions like "the economic system" as if they were concrete entities oversimplifies this complex reality and makes it seem as if there were agency and blame where there is neither.

But this is exactly the sort of fallacy committed by CRT writers when they reflexively attribute all economic disparities between races to abstractions such as "systemic racism" and "white supremacy"; for they dogmatically rule out even the possibility that some such disparities may be due instead to cultural and behavioral differences between racial groups, blaming "systemic racism" and "white supremacy" even when they cannot identify any specific racist individuals, actions, or institutions as the cause of the disparities. They are thereby fallaciously treating these abstractions as if they were concrete entities that acted to produce the disparities and can therefore be blamed for them.

Related to this is a further basic logical error, the *fallacy of division*. This involves attributing what is true of a *whole* to each of its *parts*. For instance, one would be guilty of this fallacy if he inferred, from the premise that dogs tend to be more affectionate than cats, the conclusion that any particular dog will be more affectionate than any particular cat; for what is true of dogs as a class will not necessarily be true of each individual dog. CRT writers commit this fallacy when they infer, from a premise to the effect that whites as a group enjoy "white privilege" and exhibit "white fragility", the conclusion that this or that *particular* white person enjoys "white privilege" or is exhibiting "white fragility". Even if the premise were true (which CRT gives us no good reason to believe), the conclusion wouldn't, in fact, follow.

Then there is the *fallacy of subjectivism*, which involves treating the strength of one's conviction or desire for something to be true as if it were actual evidence of its truth. Suppose, for example, that someone believes that extraterrestrials exist, for no better reason than that he finds the idea of extra-terrestrials extremely fascinating and wants there to be such things. Or imagine someone who intensely dislikes a certain co-worker, and when finding his own wallet missing one day decides that this co-worker must have been the one who took it, simply because he is, in general, such a disagreeable person. In both cases, one's feelings would be clouding one's judgment and leading one to be excessively confident in conclusions for which one has insufficient evidence.

Critical Race Theory encourages precisely this sort of fallacy insofar as one of its major themes is an emphasis on deploying "storytelling", "narrative", and "experiences" over dispassionate logical reasoning when defending CRT analyses of social problems.[11] Now, what makes stories or narratives powerful and experiences memorable are the emotions they generate. Hence to emphasize storytelling, narrative, and experiences over logical reasoning is to ensure that emotion will have a greater influence than reason will on the formation of one's beliefs. This is exacerbated by the CRT claims that racism lurks deeply in all whites, even those who sincerely claim not to be racist and are innocent of any

[11] See Delgado and Stefancic, *Critical Race Theory*, chap. 3.

overtly racist behavior, and that this alleged racism explains all inequities, even those which cannot be attributed to any specific discriminatory action or policy. This makes accusations of racism float free of any objective evidence. Accusations of "systemic racism", "micro-aggressions", "implicit bias", and the like will inevitably be grounded in the subjective feelings of the one making the accusations—feelings the intensity of which is due less to the actual facts than to the accuser's mind having been marinating in the paranoid worldview of CRT.

It is no exaggeration to say that if all the elementary logical fallacies were removed from the books of writers such as Kendi and DiAngelo, there would be hardly any argumentation left to support their claims. And the commission of these fallacies does not exhaust the basic logical errors of which they are guilty. Logic students learn that when evaluating the arguments of an opponent, intellectual honesty requires applying the "principle of charity", which tells us to consider the strongest versions of those arguments. CRT writers routinely flout this principle, casually dismissing counterarguments as racist, as expressions of "white fragility", and so on rather than seriously considering the possibility that there might be some merit to them.

Logic textbooks note that an elementary point of sound methodology is carefully to define the terms we use in an argument. This requires, among other things, avoiding circular definitions—that is, definitions that use the term being defined in the course of defining it. For example, if a political philosopher keeps talking about "freedom" and you ask him to explain exactly what he means by that, it would hardly be a helpful response for him to say that "freedom is a condition in which people are free." Kendi proves himself unable to grasp even this obvious methodological principle. For example, he defines "racist" as "one who is supporting a racist policy through their [sic] actions or inaction or expressing a racist idea".[12] "Racism", he tells us, "is a marriage of racist policies and racist ideas that produces and normalizes racial inequities."[13] An "antiracist", he informs us no less unhelpfully, is "one who is supporting an antiracist policy through their [sic] actions or expressing an antiracist idea."[14]

When he gets around to explaining what he means by "racial inequity", he tells us that it "is when two or more racial groups are not standing on approximately equal footing", and he gives as example the statistic that "71 percent of White families lived in owner-occupied homes in 2014, compared to 45 percent of Latinx [sic] families and 41 percent of Black families."[15] When you put these claims

[12] Kendi, *How to Be an Antiracist*, 13.
[13] Ibid., 17–18.
[14] Ibid., 13.
[15] Ibid., 18.

together, the result is that Kendi is simply *stipulating* that any disparity like the one he cites is "racist". This entails that his definitions violate two other standard methodological principles. For one thing, a good definition should not involve the fallacy of begging the question by simply *assuming* (as opposed to providing an argument for) a claim that is at issue between one and one's opponent. Suppose I try to convince a skeptic that I own a Ferrari by defining a "Ferrari" as a "Toyota Corolla" and then pointing out that I own a Toyota Corolla. Obviously this would not convince him, since he is unlikely to agree with this eccentric definition. Similarly, Kendi is able to "prove" that all disparities are racist simply by *defining* "racism" in a way that entails that they are. But no one who does not already agree with him would accept such a definition.

For another thing, a good definition should not be *too broad*, in the sense of including within the range of the definition things that shouldn't be there. For example, if I were to define a "car" as a "road vehicle powered by an engine", this definition would be too broad, since it would include motorcycles, which are not cars even though they are road vehicles powered by engines. Similarly, given the way Kendi defines his terms, it would follow that the fact that blacks are overrepresented in sports like basketball is racist. But Kendi himself, quite rightly, would not want to say that. Hence his definition is too broad even by his own lights.

Related to such problems is a further basic methodological failing in Critical Race Theory. Philosophers of science are agreed that an empirical claim needs to be empirically *testable*. Empirical claims are to be distinguished from claims like those made in fields such as mathematics and metaphysics, which need not be empirically testable (even though there should, of course, be some other way rationally to evaluate them). The arithmetical claim that $2 + 2 = 4$ is not the sort of thing that we can test by observation or experiment. Neither is a metaphysical claim like the thesis that there are immaterial entities (such as angels or souls); for numbers and immaterial entities are not the sorts of things one could see, hear, taste, touch, or smell, so that if we are to know one way or the other whether they exist, we have to rely on other methods.[16]

But consider claims such as *there are 350,000 species of beetles, smoking causes lung cancer, there are planets orbiting Alpha Centauri, the 1929 stock market crash triggered the Great Depression, violence on television*

[16] What methods might those be? That's a good question, but a controversial one and one that we need not address for present purposes. For discussion of the issue, see the prolegomenon of my book *Scholastic Metaphysics: A Contemporary Introduction* (Heusenstamm, Germany: Editiones Scholasticae, 2014). Some readers might be puzzled by my assertion that we cannot perceive numbers. Can't we see numbers like two and four right there on the page? No, we cannot. What we see on the page are *numerals*, which *stand for* numbers but are not the same thing as numbers. For example, the Arabic numeral "2" is no more identical with the number two than the Roman numeral "II" is.

increases the prevalence of violent behavior among youth, and the like. These are empirical claims—that is to say, claims about the observable world. Hence, in order to determine whether they are true, we need to rely on observation. In particular, we need to be able to derive *predictions* from such claims and then come up with some observational or experimental test to see if the predictions come to pass. For example, the claim that violence on television increases the prevalence of violent behavior among youth entails the prediction that if we compare groups of children who watch a lot of violent television programs with groups of children who do not, we will find there to be a higher incidence of violent behavior within the former. If this prediction is falsified, then we will have reason to judge the claim to be false.

Ever since philosopher of science Karl Popper famously called attention to *falsifiability* of this kind in the early twentieth century, it has been taken to be a hallmark of serious science (even if most contemporary philosophers of science would not endorse everything Popper said about it). Naturally, the point is not that a serious scientific theory should, in fact, have been proven false. The idea is rather that it should open itself up to falsification in the sense of making specific predictions that can be tested (where if things go well, it will pass the test and not be proven false). Popper argued that systems of belief like astrology, Freudian psychology, and Marxism are not genuinely scientific, precisely because they do not open themselves up to falsification.[17] For example, the predictions made by astrologers are typically so vague that nothing would falsify them. Suppose an astrologer tells you that *something important will happen to you next year.* Almost everyone is going to have *something* happen to him in any given year that could be said to be important; therefore, this prediction is hardly impressive. Or consider that it is hard to see what could falsify Freud's theory that much of our behavior is determined by repressed desires. If a person denies he has such desires, the denial will itself be taken as evidence that he has them! The Marxist prediction that capitalism will inevitably give way to communism is so open-ended that no matter how long capitalism lasts, the Marxist can say that the predicted revolution is still lurking around the corner. Nor is anything that happens in capitalist society taken to count as rendering the thesis even improbable. If the condition of the working class worsens, the Marxist will say that this is a result of capitalist exploitation and will eventually trigger revolution. But if the condition of the working class improves due to social welfare measures, the

[17] Cf. Karl R. Popper, "Science: Conjectures and Refutations", in Popper's *Conjectures and Refutations: The Growth of Scientific Knowledge* (New York: Harper and Row, 1968).

Marxist will say that such measures are a stratagem by which the capitalist class temporarily prolongs its power and can at most only delay the inevitable revolution.

The central claims of Critical Race Theory are no more falsifiable, and therefore no more testable, than the claims of these other belief systems. Racism is said by writers such as Kendi and DiAngelo to lurk in every white person, even those who exhibit no overtly racist behavior and who sincerely think of themselves as opposed to racism. Their denial that they are racists is taken only to confirm that they are racists, denial being "the heartbeat of racism" in Kendi's view and a manifestation of "white fragility" in DiAngelo's. Bell claims that even legal reforms usually cited as great advances in the fight *against* racism really function only to *uphold* racism. Bell and CRT writers also hold that color-blindness and race-neutrality, traditionally regarded as definitive of *opposition* to racism, are, in fact, racist as well. In these ways, all the obvious evidence that racism has massively decreased in recent decades is simply conjured away.

Meanwhile, Freeman says that even to approach the question of disparities by seeking to identify specific individuals or actions which might be responsible for them reflects the perspective of the "perpetrators" of racism. Similarly, Crenshaw dismisses as irrelevant the question whether disparities were intentionally produced. Hence the inability of CRT writers to prove that all disparities are the result of racism is also explained away. Racism is instead simply *defined* by CRT writers in such a way that disparities are the result of racism, and even the suggestion that there might be some alternative explanation is dismissed *a priori* as racist—though this is true only in cases where it is whites who are better off. In the case of disparities where blacks, Asians, or other nonwhites are better off than whites, CRT writers do *not* attribute the outcome to racism.

Thus is the game rigged so that everything can be interpreted as evidence for CRT and nothing can be allowed to count against it. "Heads, CRT wins; tails, critics of CRT lose." Critical Race Theory is thereby made unfalsifiable, but, for that reason, also unverifiable; for since it makes no testable predictions, it cannot pass any evidential test. At the same time, its ideological stacking of the deck gives it the false *appearance* of having evidence in its favor. Psychologists and other social scientists have labeled this phenomenon "confirmation bias"—the tendency to search out evidence that seems to confirm one's preexisting beliefs, to ignore potential sources of evidence against them, and to interpret all ambiguous evidence in one's favor. CRT essentially trains its adepts, not to avoid confirmation bias, but precisely to engage in it on a massive scale.

6

Social Scientific Objections to Critical Race Theory

Considered from the point of view of general methodology, then, Critical Race Theory is simply abysmal social science. This judgment is greatly reinforced when we consider what the empirical evidence, looked at without the ideological CRT lenses, actually shows about some of its specific claims. Again, CRT writers routinely treat economic and other disparities as if they could have no explanation other than racism, and they also treat such disparities, and the discrimination and other injustices that are alleged to be their cause, as if they were essentially coterminous with "white supremacy". But as economist Thomas Sowell has shown, none of this stands up to scrutiny.[1]

[1] See Thomas Sowell, *Intellectuals and Race* (New York: Basic Books, 2013), especially chap. 2. Sowell treats these issues in greater detail in *Discrimination and Disparities*, rev. ed. (New York: Basic Books, 2019).

For example, in the United States it is often pointed out that with respect to jobs, income, mortgage approval rates, credit scores, and the like, whites fare better than blacks. This is then attributed to racial discrimination. But the same statistics show that Asian Americans do better than whites, and that black-owned banks turn down black mortgage applicants at a higher rate than white-owned banks do.[2] Yet these facts are not attributed to racial discrimination, and they certainly count against the "white supremacy" thesis. If the economic system was rigged so as to favor whites, why would Asian Americans do better than whites? If antiblack racism was the reason for the economic differences between whites and blacks, why would black-owned banks turn down black applicants even more frequently than white-owned banks do? (Critical Race Theorists would no doubt attempt to explain the latter by alleging that blacks have picked up a self-defeating antiblack animus from the surrounding white supremacist culture. But the problem is that there is no *evidence* for this claim; it is simply an *ad hoc* hypothesis designed to rescue CRT from refutation by the actual empirical evidence.)

Critical Race Theory assumes that the default position in human affairs is that all racial and ethnic groups will be at parity with respect to economic

[2] Sowell, *Intellectuals and Race*, 4–5.

prosperity, proportional representation in various fields of endeavor, and so on, and that where there are disparities it must be because racial discrimination has prevented groups from achieving this parity. But as Sowell shows, the actual evidence of human history goes massively against both of these assumptions. For one thing, few if any societies in history have ever even approximated, much less achieved, proportional representation or economic parity between groups.[3] So what actual *evidence* is there to believe that proportional representation and economic parity is the natural or default situation? For another thing, there are a great many cases where racial discrimination could not possibly have been the reason for disparities and a variety of alternative factors clearly were responsible.

In particular, and as Sowell notes, there are many examples in history of minority groups who have *economically* outperformed majorities that were *politically* dominant, so that discrimination could hardly be the explanation of this outperformance.[4] For instance, in the Ottoman Empire's capital Istanbul near the beginning of the twentieth century, non-Turks and non-Muslims dominated banking and finance, and Greeks and Armenians had disproportionate control over industry. Writes Sowell: "The

[3] Ibid., 10.
[4] Ibid., 8–9.

racial or ethnic minorities who have owned or
directed more than half of whole industries in particular nations have included the Chinese in Malay-
sia, the Lebanese in West Africa, Greeks in the
Ottoman Empire, Britons in Argentina, Belgians
in Russia, Jews in Poland, and Spanish in Chile—
among many others."[5] At different periods, the
Tamil minority has dominated the medical profession in Ceylon, German and Japanese minorities
dominated various industries in São Paulo, Brazil,
the Indian minority dominated the cotton industry in Uganda, and Italian immigrants looking for
loans were especially favored by bankers in Argentina and the United States. And so on. In each of
these cases it would be ridiculous to suggest that the
economic system was somehow rigged in favor of
the successful minority groups and against the politically dominant and less successful majority—that
somehow there must have been "systemic racism"
that favored "Greek supremacy" in the Ottoman
Empire, or "Tamil supremacy" in Ceylon, or "Italian supremacy" in the United States. Or, consider
the overrepresentation of Jews in the arts and sci-
ences and other fields by the middle of the twentieth century—despite being subject to extreme
persecution and despite first-generation Jewish
immigrants often being impoverished.[6] Was this the

[5] Ibid., 8.
[6] Sowell, *Discrimination and Disparities*, 11.

consequence of "Jewish supremacy" or "systemic anti-Gentile" policy? Only an anti-Semite would believe such nonsense. But it is no less nonsensical to assert dogmatically that disparities in the contemporary United States simply *must* be the product of "white supremacy" (especially given that, as already noted, Asian Americans outperform whites in various respects).

Many who comment on these issues suppose that if discrimination is not the explanation for such disparities, then genetics must be the only alternative. But as Sowell emphasizes, this is a false choice. Economic and other social outcomes are typically complex, the consequences of a large number of factors. An outcome may have several prerequisites, such that the absence of any one of them will prevent the outcome from occurring, even if the others are present—and its absence may have nothing to do with either discrimination or genetics.[7] Where the historical differences in degree of prosperity between nations are concerned, factors might include relative geographical isolation or easy access to trading partners, the presence or absence of natural harbors, availability of beasts of burden or lack thereof, contingencies such as the outcome of a battle, and so on.[8] Another factor could be the median age of a group, insofar as the population

[7] Ibid., 1–6.
[8] Sowell, *Intellectuals and Race*, 10–18.

of a group with a higher median age is bound to
embody a higher aggregate level of experience,
knowledge, and skills of various kinds.[9] Moreover,
if a nation comes to have an advantage in a certain
area of endeavor, its people are bound to carry it
with them when they emigrate. Thus did German
immigrants come to have an outsize influence in the
beer industry in the United States, Argentina, and
Brazil, and Jewish immigrants from Europe would
become prominent in the apparel industry in the
United States and Argentina.[10]

As these last examples indicate, another crucial
factor is *culture*—the values, beliefs, customs, habits, and the like shared by a people and passed on
from generation to generation. Indeed, historian
and economist David Landes judges that "culture
makes almost all the difference" to the economic
outcomes enjoyed by a group.[11] Because culture
is relatively stable, its economic consequences will
also be relatively stable over time, so that groups
with cultural practices more conducive to economic prosperity will tend to retain their economic

[9] Ibid., 16.

[10] Ibid., 15.

[11] David Landes, "Culture Makes Almost All the Difference", in
Lawrence E. Harrison and Samuel P. Huntington, eds., *Culture Mat-
ters: How Values Shape Human Progress* (New York: Basic Books, 2000).
See also Landes' book *The Wealth and Poverty of Nations* (New York:
Norton, 1998).

advantages over other groups over time. Still, culture can change, and when it does it can yield a change in the economic fortunes of a group—such cultural change often being the missing prerequisite among the multiple ingredients which, as Sowell emphasizes, are often necessary for certain economic outcomes. Landes discusses the example of Japan's sudden rise to industrial modernization and economic power during the nineteenth century.[12] Some of the prerequisites were in place, such as effective government, a high literacy rate, tight family structure, an ethic of self-discipline and work, and a strong sense of national identity. But there was also a new willingness to open Japan to influences from the outside, and in particular a determination to study and adopt the industrial and economic practices that had worked for other groups, especially the English and the Germans.

Landes also defends Max Weber's famous thesis that the rise of modern capitalism was largely a byproduct of the Protestant Reformation.[13] While Protestants rejected the idea that one could *earn* one's salvation by good works, living a moral life was nevertheless often seen as a reassuring sign that one has indeed been saved. As the relevant theological presuppositions faded with the rise of secularism, the

[12] Landes, "Culture Makes Almost All the Difference", 7–10.
[13] Ibid., 11–13.

moral ideal morphed into the notion that a respectable life was one characterized by bourgeois virtues such as honesty, hard work, earnestness, thrift, and the good use of one's time. Together with the rise in literacy entailed by the Protestant emphasis on every believer's need to read Scripture for himself, these values made for a culture highly favorable to business and accumulation of capital.

Cameroonian economist Daniel Etounga-Manguelle argues that the cultural values that tend to predominate in African societies are *not* as favorable to business and capital accumulation, and that this accounts for the economic disparities between African and Western countries.[14] African societies, he says, tend to be oriented toward the past and preserving what has been handed on by one's ancestors, rather than to the future and imagining new possibilities. As a result, they tend to regard the status quo as immutable and are, accordingly, not inclined toward long-range planning or working for the attainment of distant goals. They also tend to see social arrangements in hierarchical and static terms rather than in terms of the egalitarian and dynamic view of one's position in society that prevails in the West. Going along with this, says Etounga-Manguelle, is a tendency to see the interests of the

[14] Daniel Etounga-Manguelle, "Does Africa Need a Cultural Adjustment Program?", in Harrison and Huntington, *Culture Matters*.

individual as subordinate to those of the family and
the community more generally, to see authority as
deriving more from the power of particular rulers
than from abstract laws, and to give little place to
an attitude of skepticism toward established ways.
There is also an emphasis on conviviality, socia-
bility, and pleasure over efficiency and work. All
of this goes against the grain of the individualistic,
entrepreneurial, and careerist spirit of modern capitalist societies.

It is crucial to emphasize that the point is *not* that
the cultural attitudes Landes describes are good and
the ones that Etounga-Manguelle describes are bad.
Far from it. From a Catholic point of view, there is
much to criticize in the first and much to praise in
the second. African Catholics are justly known to
be more loyal to the traditional teaching and Magis-
terium of the Church than their Western brethren,
and the values summarized by Etounga-Manguelle
obviously facilitate this. Western capitalist societies,
meanwhile, are not only more secular, but prone to
vapid consumerism and other aspects of what Pope
Saint John Paul II condemned as "economism".
The accumulation of wealth, economic efficiency,
technological innovation, and the like are by no
means the highest human values, so that a culture
that facilitates them is not *ipso facto* superior to others, full stop. It may, all things considered, even be
inferior to others.

At the same time, if we are looking *just* at disparate economic outcomes between nations and ethnic groups, it is simply not reasonable to deny that different cultural attitudes and habits play a major role. Lawrence Harrison identifies ten values that set what he labels "progressive" cultures apart from "static" ones and account for the former's greater economic prosperity.[15] First, progressive cultures are oriented toward the future and emphasize control over one's own destiny, whereas static cultures focus on the present or the past. Second, progressive cultures idealize work and see in it personal satisfaction as well as financial rewards, whereas static cultures see work as a burden. Third, progressive cultures emphasize frugality and investment for the future, whereas static cultures distrust them as undermining the egalitarian status quo and tend to look at economics as a zero-sum game. Fourth, progressive cultures emphasize education as a key to progress, whereas static cultures regard it as unimportant except for the elite members of society. Fifth, advancement in progressive cultures follows from merit, whereas in static cultures it is family and connections that count. Sixth, in progressive cultures the radii of trust and economic interaction

[15] Lawrence E. Harrison, "Promoting Progressive Cultural Change", in Harrison and Huntington, eds., *Culture Matters*. See also Harrison's book *Who Prospers? How Cultural Values Shape Economic and Political Success* (New York: Basic Books, 1992).

with others extend across all individuals, whereas in static cultures they are more tightly confined to one's own family or tribe. Seventh, progressive cultures have an ethical code that strongly condemns corruption, nepotism, and the like, whereas static cultures are more tolerant of such practices. Eighth, and relatedly, impersonal standards of justice and fair play (as opposed to connections or ability to pay) are more widely respected and insisted upon in progressive cultures than in static ones. Ninth, authority tends to be more dispersed in progressive cultures and more concentrated in static ones. Tenth and finally, progressive cultures tend to be more secular and skeptical, static cultures more religious and conformist.

Harrison acknowledges that his characterization is idealized and that few if any cultures are entirely "progressive" or "static" in his senses of those terms. Naturally, one could also quibble about some of the details of his account. But it would be absurd to deny that a culture that more closely approximates what he calls "progressive" attitudes and habits is bound to be more prosperous economically than one that more closely approximates what he calls "static" attitudes and habits. Again, that does not entail that such a culture is *better*, all things considered. The point is simply that cultural differences clearly play a major role in explaining economic disparities between some groups. There is plainly no basis for insisting that discrimination or "systemic racism" *must* be the explanation. And while a reasonable person could, of course, try to develop counterarguments against the views of social scientists Sowell, Landes, Etounga-Manguelle, and Harrison, the problem is that writers such as Kendi and DiAngelo do not develop counterarguments. Rather, they dogmatically dismiss as "racist" even the suggestion that cultural differences, rather than racism, might explain economic disparities.

What about other factors emphasized by Critical Race Theorists, such as colonialism? That colonialism is insufficient to explain why some former colonies are economically worse off than Western capitalist countries should be obvious from the fact that this is not true of all former colonies. Singapore and Hong Kong are former British colonies, and Taiwan and South Korea are former Japanese colonies, and all of them have thrived economically.[16] Ghanaian economist George Ayittey points out that in at least some African countries, the former colonial powers actually left behind crucial infrastructure such as roads, hospitals, universities, telephone systems, civil service, and the like—and that these resources fell into grave disrepair only long *after* the colonizers departed.[17] As Ayittey notes, it is the

[16] Lawrence E. Harrison, introduction to Harrison and Huntington, eds., *Culture Matters*, xx.

[17] George B. N. Ayittey, *Africa in Chaos* (New York: St. Martin's, 1998), 41–42.

socialist and other statist economic systems that so many African countries adopted after independence that is the most obvious cause of their economic woes.[18] To be sure, this was itself, in part, a consequence of colonialism; for some colonial powers administered their colonies in a statist manner, and post-colonial socialist African governments preserved and deepened this statism. Some postcolonial African leaders also picked up a hostility to capitalism while studying in Western universities. This is not an aspect of the colonial inheritance that CRT adepts are likely to want to emphasize, however, since they tend to be anticapitalist themselves.[19]

By far the most important cultural factor influencing disparate group outcomes is the relative stability of the family. That is precisely what we should expect, given that the family is the fundamental social unit, such that larger groups can hardly prosper when it is weak, any more than a body can be healthy when its organs are sick. As the *Catechism of the Catholic Church* teaches, "The family is *the original cell of social life. . . .* Authority, stability, and

[18] Ibid.,112–18.

[19] See Ibram X. Kendi, *How to Be an Antiracist* (New York: One World, 2019), 156–63. It should be added that socialism is not an extension of African cultural values, contrary to what some postcolonial African socialist leaders claimed. As Ayittey argues, in traditional African society it is not the individual that is the fundamental economic and social unit, but neither is it the state or society as a whole. Rather, it is the extended family, and family ownership is a kind of private ownership.

a life of relationships within the family constitute the foundations for freedom, security, and fraternity within society" (2207). Pope Pius XI taught:

> As history testifies, the prosperity of the State and the temporal happiness of its citizens cannot remain safe and sound where the foundation on which they are established, which is the moral order, is weakened and where the very fountainhead from which the State draws its life, namely, wedlock and the family, is obstructed by the vices of its citizens.[20]

Similarly, the *Compendium of the Social Doctrine of the Church* says:

> It is patently clear that the good of persons and the proper functioning of society are closely connected "with the healthy state of conjugal and family life." Without families that are strong in their communion and stable in their commitment peoples grow weak. In the family, moral values are taught starting from the very first years of life, the spiritual heritage of the religious community and the cultural legacy of the nation are transmitted. In the family one learns social responsibility and solidarity.[21]

---

[20] Pius XI, encyclical letter *Casti Connubii* (December 31, 1930), no. 123.

[21] *Compendium*, no. 213, quoting *GS*, 47: *AAS* 58 (1966), 1067; cf. *Catechism of the Catholic Church*, no. 2210, hereafter, *Catechism*.

The obvious corollary is that social groups in which marriage and family are weak are bound to function less well than those in which they are strong; are less likely effectively to pass on moral, religious, and cultural values; and are less likely to produce children that have learned social responsibility and solidarity. Economic and other disparities are bound to result.

This is all common sense, but social science confirms it if there were any doubt. Sociologist David Popenoe is one of several prominent researchers who have studied the catastrophic effects of widespread fatherlessness and the having of children out of wedlock.[22] Of families headed by mothers, he says, "no other group is so poor, and none stays poor longer", and "the children of mother-headed families are the very poorest of the poor."[23] This outcome has been especially hard on black American families and children. Popenoe writes:

> The loss of fathers' income, of course, is not the only reason for the recent growth of child poverty

[22] David Popenoe, *Life Without Father: Compelling New Evidence That Fatherhood and Marriage Are Indispensable for the Good of Children and Society* (New York: Free Press, 1996). See also David Blankenhorn, *Fatherless America: Confronting Our Most Urgent Social Problem* (New York: HarperPerennial, 1996), and James Q. Wilson, *The Marriage Problem: How Our Culture Has Weakened Families* (New York: HarperCollins, 2002).

[23] Popenoe, *Life Without Father*, 54 and 55.

in America. But it is the predominant reason. By one estimate, 51 percent of the increase in child poverty observed during the 1980s (65 percent for blacks) can be attributed to changes in family structure. Indeed, much of the income differential between whites and blacks today, perhaps as much as two thirds, can be attributed to the differences in family structure.[24]

Nor are bad economic outcomes the only dire effects. Popenoe notes that children in single-parent families are significantly more likely to suffer from emotional and behavioral problems and to do poorly in school.[25] Girls who grow up without their biological fathers are more likely to be sexually active and to become pregnant out of wedlock themselves, and the problem is not mitigated when stepfathers are present. Moreover, stepfathers and mothers' boyfriends are more likely to inflict physical and sexual abuse (even though, of course, most do not do so) than natural fathers, and in general, child abuse occurs more frequently in households from which the biological father is absent.[26]

Then there is the effect of fatherlessness on crime. As Popenoe notes, "Juvenile delinquency and violence are clearly generated disproportionately by youths in mother-only households and in

[24] Ibid., 54.
[25] Ibid., 56–57.
[26] Ibid., 65–73.

other households where the biological father is not present."[27] This is especially true of young men. Popenoe writes:

> Sixty percent of America's rapists, 72 percent of adolescent murderers, and 70 percent of long-term prison inmates come from fatherless homes.... [T]his is no statistical artifact. Fathers are important to their sons as role models. They are important for maintaining authority and discipline. And they are important in helping their sons to develop both self-control and feelings of empathy toward others, character traits that are found to be lacking in violent youth.[28]

Moreover, fatherless young men who fail to form attachments to wife and children of their own are far more prone to violence, drug use, and other antisocial and risky behaviors. As Popenoe argues, it will not do to attribute these behaviors to lack of jobs. Rather, it is the responsibility for wife and children that acts as a civilizing force on young men, leading them to avoid dangerous behavior and seek employment.[29]

Fatherlessness and having children out of wedlock generate these bad effects *whatever* the race of those involved. But the proportion of single-parent

[27] Ibid., 62.
[28] Ibid., 63.
[29] Ibid., 75.

families among black Americans is larger than the proportion among whites, and the proportion among whites is larger than the proportion among Asian Americans.[30] This fact affords an obvious cultural explanation of the economic and other disparities that hold between these groups. Yet writers like Kendi not only dogmatically prefer to attribute such disparities to racism, but into the bargain attribute this alternative explanation to "racist patriarchs" whose call for a renewal of black fatherhood is "sexist".[31] This is simply to double down on ideological *ad hominem* distractions from uncomfortable empirical evidence.

Some acknowledge the dire economic and social effects of fatherlessness, but nevertheless attribute it to racism insofar as it is, they suggest, a lingering effect of slavery. But Sowell argues that this idea does not withstand scrutiny:

> The fact that so many black families today consist of women with fatherless children has been said by many to be a legacy of slavery. Yet most black children grew up in two-parent families, even under slavery itself, and for generations thereafter. As recently as 1960, two-thirds of black children were still living in two-parent families. A century ago,

---

[30] "Children in Single-Parent Families by Race in the United States", Kids Count Data Center (2019), https://datacenter.kidscount.org/. Accessed September 29, 2021.

[31] Kendi, *How to Be an Antiracist*, 183–84.

a slightly higher percentage of blacks were mar-
ried than were whites.... The reasons for changes
for the worse in these and other patterns must be
sought in our own times. Whatever the reasons for
the disintegration of the black family, it escalated
to the current disastrous level well over a century
after the end of slavery, though less than a generation after a large expansion of the welfare state and
its accompanying non-judgmental ideology.[32]

Not coincidentally, the expansion and ideology
Sowell refers to appeared at the same time as the
sexual revolution. And such factors reinforce Sowell's point that genetic explanations of disparities
are not the only alternatives to explanations that
attribute disparities to racism. *Cultural* changes can
generate disparities, and when they do the remedy
is to reverse those changes. Yet despite the enor-
mous harm it has manifestly done to black families,
the sexual revolution is not something CRT writers are interested in rolling back. On the contrary,
via the notion of "intersectionality", they fold the
cause of so-called sexual liberation into their brand
of antiracism.

There are yet other problems that social science
poses for Critical Race Theory. CRT writers often
hold that even those who sincerely claim not to be
racist nevertheless harbor unconscious prejudices

[32] Sowell, *Intellectuals and Race*, 120–21.

in the form of "implicit bias". They allege that subtle prejudices frequently give rise to "micro-aggressions" against members of racial minority groups. But is there any actual empirical evidence for these claims? There is not, and attempts by social scientists to establish them have been seriously problematic. In the case of implicit bias, there are several persistent problems with psychological tests that purport to reveal its existence.[33] For one thing, it is not clear that the bias that researchers are attempting to detect is really any different from the *explicit* biases we are already familiar with. There is evidence that subjects of tests for implicit bias can predict how they are likely to do and adjust their answers accordingly—in which case, how are their purported biases of the exotic *implicit* kind? For another thing, subjects frequently get different results when retaking the test, which indicates that the results may reflect more about the test and the circumstances in which it is given than about any stable traits of the person taking it. Such tests also turn out to be poor predictors of actual behavior outside the testing context. Indeed, in some cases those whom the tests purportedly show to harbor

[33] See Edouard Machery, "Anomalies in implicit attitudes research", *Wiley Interdisciplinary Reviews: Cognitive Science* (June 15, 2021), and the social scientific literature surveyed in Jonathan D. Church, *Reinventing Racism: Why "White Fragility" Is the Wrong Way to Think about Racial Inequality* (Lanham, Md.: Rowman and Littlefield, 2021), chap. 2.

implicit bias appear to be *more* inclined to behave positively toward members of minority groups (perhaps precisely out of fear of being thought biased).[34] Then there is the fact that what counts as "bias" is not easy to determine in a scientifically rigorous way. It would hardly be useful to define it in a way that presupposes the claims of Critical Race Theory (e.g., in terms of disagreement with the thesis that all disparities are of their nature racist), since this would simply beg the question in favor of CRT rather than provide independent scientific confirmation of it.

As a recent survey of the literature found, the concept of "microaggressions" is no better supported by any actual social scientific research.[35] Attempts to establish the prevalence of microaggressions are typically based on sample sizes too small to be statistically interesting. The subjective reactions of the researchers themselves tend to determine what counts as a "microaggression", and confirmation bias is thus what leads them to see microaggressions in their samples. Even then, the studies fail to establish that members of minority groups would themselves agree with the researchers about whether some behavior amounts to a "microaggression".

[34] Church, *Reinventing Racism*, 24–25.
[35] See Edward Cantu and Lee Jussim, "Microaggressions, Questionable Science, and Free Speech", *Texas Review of Law and Politics* (April 16, 2021).

Not only is there no evidence for the existence of implicit bias, microaggressions, and other presumed exotic forms of racism, but as Greg Lukianoff and Jonathan Haidt have pointed out, seeing the world through the lenses of such CRT concepts can actually do serious damage to mental health.[36] Cognitive Behavioral Therapy (or CBT), as they note, is widely acknowledged to be among the most effective methods for treating depression, anxiety, obsessive compulsive disorder, and the like. Among the factors that lead to such disorders are a number of cognitive distortions or bad habits of thinking that incline us to misperceive our environment and exaggerate or invent difficulties. These include *emotional reasoning*, or letting our feelings determine how we interpret reality rather than letting reality determine whether our feelings are the appropriate ones; *catastrophizing*, or focusing obsessively on the imagined worst possible outcome rather than on what the evidence shows are more likely outcomes; *overgeneralizing*, or jumping to sweeping conclusions on the basis of one or a few incidents; *dichotomous thinking*, or seeing things in either-or terms when a more sober analysis would reveal more possibilities; *mind reading*, or jumping to conclusions about what other people are thinking; *labeling*, or slapping

[36] Greg Lukianoff and Jonathan Haidt, *The Coddling of the American Mind: How Good Intentions and Bad Ideas Are Setting Up a Generation for Failure* (New York: Penguin, 2018), chap. 2.

a simplistic description on some person or phenomenon that papers over its complexity; *negative filtering*
and *discounting positives*, or looking only for confirming evidence for some pessimistic assumption while
denying or downplaying confirming evidence that
things are not in fact so bad; and *blaming*, or focusing
on others as the sources of one's negative feelings
rather than taking responsibility for them oneself.

Obviously, the more thoroughly one is prone to
these habits of thought, the more likely one is to see
the world in excessively negative terms and to be
miserable as a result. CBT thus aims to help patients
identify these bad mental habits and to counteract
them. But Critical Race Theory positively encourages all of these cognitive distortions. It teaches
emotional reasoning insofar as it pits personal "narratives" against the ideals of rationality and objectivity, and insofar as it makes the subjective reactions
of offended people the measure of whether they
are victims of "microaggressions". It encourages
blaming by treating accusations about microaggressions and other grievances as if they can never
reasonably be regarded as stemming from over-
sensitivity or paranoia on the part of the person
offended. It indulges in negative filtering and discounting positives insofar as it arbitrarily defines
"racism" so broadly that anything can be made to
count as racist, even what would historically have
been regarded as major advances in the fight against

racism (such as color-blind or race-neutral policies and opposition to all racial discrimination). In the same way, it engages in labeling, by ignoring all the complex causes of disparities and the different motives behind various actions and policies, and simply slapping the description "racist" on them. It promotes dichotomous thinking insofar as it insists that one either agrees with CRT or ought to be dismissed as "racist". It exhibits catastrophizing in that it denies that anything short of implementing the most extreme of CRT policy recommendations will leave us with a racist society that has made little if any real progress since the days of segregation. It encourages mind reading by imputing "implicit bias", "white fragility", and other racist attitudes to all whites, even in the absence of any objective evidence for these attributions. It overgeneralizes by treating any particular case of a real or perceived racial injustice as if it amounted to confirmation of the entire extremist CRT worldview.

In short, Critical Race Theory positively encourages paranoid habits of mind analogous to those exhibited by people suffering from depression and anxiety. Looking at the world through CRT lenses leads one to see racism even where it does not exist, to feel strongly aggrieved at this imagined racism, and then to treat the narrative of grievance that results as if it were confirming evidence of the reality of the imagined racism. As a result, much of the general public has, under the influence of Kendi's and DiAngelo's bestsellers and other CRT-inspired propaganda, come to have a massively distorted perception of race relations and the incidence of racist behavior in contemporary American society.

Political scientist Eric Kaufmann has gathered some of the relevant evidence.[37] He notes the dramatic decline in racist attitudes and behavior over the last several decades:

> The share of white Americans who agree that it is permissible to racially discriminate when selling a home declined from 60% as late as 1980 to 28% by 2012. Approval of black-white intermarriage rose among whites from around 4% in 1958 to 45% in 1995 and 84% in 2013, according to Gallup. In 2017, fewer than 10% of whites in a major Pew survey said that interracial marriage was a "bad thing".... Meanwhile, police killings of African-Americans declined by 60%–80% from the late 1960s to the early 2000s and have remained at this level ever since.[38]

Yet increasing numbers of people on the left side of the political spectrum have come to believe that the prevalence of racism is increasing. Kaufmann notes that the percentage of white liberals who regarded

---

[37] Eric Kaufmann, *The Social Construction of Racism in the United States* (New York: The Manhattan Institute, 2021).

[38] Ibid., 9.

racism as a serious problem went from under 40 percent in 2014 to over 80 percent in 2017.[39] This occurred precisely at a time when Critical Race Theory and other "woke" ideas began to influence mainstream liberal politics, especially through social media. Exposure to such media evidently affects people's perceptions even of their own circumstances, let alone of the state of race relations in society as a whole. As Kaufmann notes, "Black respondents on social media in 2016 were considerably more likely to report experiencing discrimination than those not on social media."[40]

Ideology and social media also have a dramatic effect on public perceptions of the attitudes of police toward minority groups. For example, media coverage of several high-profile cases has led many greatly to exaggerate the incidence of police violence against black Americans. As Kaufmann writes:

> Eight in 10 African-American survey respondents believe that young black men are more likely to be shot to death by the police than to die in a traffic accident; one in 10 disagrees. Among a highly educated sample of liberal whites, more than six in 10 agreed. In reality, considerably more young African-American men die in car accidents than are shot to death by police....

[39] Ibid., 18.
[40] Ibid., 10.

Only about a fifth of liberals but close to half of conservatives gave the right answer to a question on how many unarmed black men were killed by police in 2019. Fully 54% of "very liberal" Americans thought that more than 1,000 were killed compared with the actual figure of between 13 and 27.[41]

Or consider the killing of George Floyd by police officer Derek Chauvin, which led to riots that caused twenty-five deaths and over $1 billion in property damage, and to Critical Race Theory's sudden and unprecedented publicity and influence. Many assume the killing to have been obviously racially motivated. Yet when asked why prosecutors did not charge Chauvin with a hate crime, Minnesota Attorney General Keith Ellison, who is black and politically liberal, said: "I wouldn't call it that because hate crimes are crimes where there's an explicit motive ... of bias. We don't have any evidence that Derek Chauvin factored in George Floyd's race as he did what he did."[42] Ellison attributed Chauvin's actions instead to arrogance, and in particular to a refusal to listen to the crowd that was warning him that his excessive restraint on Floyd's neck was putting Floyd's life in danger.

[41] Ibid., 5 and 16.

[42] Interview on *60 Minutes*, June 20, 2021, https://www.cbsnews.com/news/derek-chauvin-prosecutors-george-floyd-death-60-minutes-2021-06-20/.

While he agreed that race plays a role in the different ways police sometimes treat different citizens, Ellison emphasized that other factors, such as class, are often more significant:

> If an officer doesn't throw a white neurologist in Eden Prairie, Minnesota to the ground and doesn't sit on top of his neck, is he doing it because this is a fellow white brother? No. He's doing it because he thinks, "This is an important person and if I treat them badly somebody's going to ask me about this. This person probably has lawyers. He probably knows the governor. He probably knows—he has connections. I can look at the way he's dressed and the way he talks, that he's probably, quote, unquote, 'somebody.'" And so that's really what it's about.[43]

Floyd's killing was a grave injustice, and even if it was not racially motivated, that does not entail that race plays no role in other cases of police brutality. But that simply does not show that we should accept Critical Race Theory, any more than the reality of economic injustices shows that we should embrace Marxism. CRT's extreme claims are in no way supported by any empirical evidence. Rather, they are read *into* the evidence by ideologues whose thinking is, as we have seen, highly influenced by various cognitive distortions and logical fallacies.

[43] Ibid.

7

Catholicism versus Critical Race Theory

As noted already, Critical Race Theory essentially reformulates, in racial terms, some of the key themes of Marxism and postmodernism. Now, the Church has consistently and strenuously condemned the key ideas of Marxism and all other forms of socialism and communism, along with the relativist and other themes that are characteristic of postmodernism. It follows that CRT, which is a mere variation on these malign ideas, is no more compatible with the teaching of the Church than Marxism and postmodernism are.

For example, the Church has condemned the Marxist thesis that social classes, such as the rich and the poor or capital and labor, are inherently and necessarily hostile to one another. For instance, in *Rerum Novarum*, Pope Leo XIII describes this thesis as "abhorrent to reason and truth" and insists that in reality "nature has commanded ... that the ...

classes mentioned should agree harmoniously and should properly form equally balanced counterparts to each other" (28). It can hardly be less abhorrent to hold, as CRT does, that "antiblackness" is intrinsic to "white identity" such that the relationship between whites and nonwhites is inherently one of oppressor and oppressed. CRT race analysis is as divisive and contrary to social harmony as Marxist class analysis is, and the CRT demonization of "whiteness" is therefore no more compatible with Catholic social teaching than is the Marxist demonization of the "bourgeois" and of "capital". And it is potentially just as violent as the latter has proved to be. Indeed, one CRT-influenced writer, in a book that got much attention and even some praise in the mainstream press, has defended rioting and looting in the name of antiracism.[1]

While the Church commands the rich to come to the assistance of the poor, she also makes it clear that this has nothing to do with the socialist goal of equalizing outcomes. For though the distinction is often blurred in political rhetoric, there is a difference between eliminating poverty and eliminating inequality. There is also a difference between affirming that human beings are equal in their dignity and basic rights, and claiming that they ought

---

[1] Vicky Osterweil, *In Defense of Looting* (New York: Bold Type Books, 2020).

all to have the same amount of wealth, ought all to be equally represented in each profession, and so forth. Indeed, the Church has repeatedly condemned the thesis that inequalities in wealth and the like are intrinsically unjust. In *Rerum Novarum*, Pope Leo XIII teaches:

> It is impossible to reduce civil society to one dead level. Socialists may in that intent do their utmost, but all striving against nature is in vain. There naturally exist among mankind manifold differences of the most important kind; people differ in capacity, skill, health, strength; and unequal fortune is a necessary result of unequal condition. (17)

And in *Humanum Genus*, the pope writes:

> No one doubts that all men are equal one to another, so far as regards their common origin and nature, or the last end which each one has to attain, or the rights and duties which are thence derived. But, as the abilities of all are not equal, as one differs from another in the powers of mind or body, and as there are very many dissimilarities of manner, disposition, and character, it is most repugnant to reason to endeavor to confine all within the same measure, and to extend complete equality to the institutions of civic life. (26)

Pope Saint Pius X taught the same. Criticizing the Sillonist religious socialist movement in the encyclical *Notre Charge Apostolique*, he writes:

The Sillon says that it is striving to establish an era
of equality which, by that very fact, would be also
an era of greater justice. Thus, to the Sillon, every
inequality of condition is an injustice, or at least,
a diminution of justice. Here we have a principle that conflicts sharply with the nature of things,
a principle conducive to jealously, injustice, and
subversive to any social order.

This teaching appears in yet other writings of
these popes, and was reiterated by Pope Pius XI and
Pope Pius XII.[2] In line with this traditional teaching, the 1988 Pontifical Commission on Justice
and Peace document *The Church and Racism*, while
affirming that "no human group ... can boast of
having a natural superiority over others", also states:

If people and human communities are all equal in
dignity, that does not mean that they all have, at
a given moment, equal physical abilities, cultural
endowments, intellectual and moral strengths, or
that they are at the same stage of development.
Equality does not mean uniformity. It is important
to recognize the diversity and complementarity of

[2] Cf. Leo XIII, encyclical letter *Quod Apostolici Muneris* (December
28, 1878), no. 9; Pius X, motu proprio *Fin Dalla Prima* (December 18,
1903); Pius XI, encyclical letter *Divini Redemptoris* (March 19, 1937),
no. 33; and Pius XII, address (June 4, 1953), quoted in Ronald J.
Rychlak, "Pope Pius XII on Social Issues", in *Catholic Social Teaching:
A Volume of Scholarly Essays*, eds. Gerard V. Bradley and E. Christian
Brugger (Cambridge: Cambridge University Press, 2019), 132.

one another's cultural riches and moral qualities. Equality of treatment therefore implies a certain recognition of differences which minorities themselves demand in order to develop according to their own specific characteristics, in respect for others and for the common good of society and the world community. (23)

Nor is it just radical egalitarianism concerning material conditions that the Church rejects. The Church also condemns the claim that all *cultures* are equally good in every important respect, along with the relativist thesis that there are no objective standards outside of cultures by reference to which they might be judged. Pope Saint Paul VI condemned "the rise of a depraved moral relativism, one that clearly endangers the Church's entire doctrinal heritage".[3] Pope Saint John Paul II also warned of "the dangers of relativism",[4] and Pope Benedict XVI of "a dictatorship of relativism".[5] The Old Testament repeatedly condemns the cultures of the peoples surrounding ancient Israel for their moral and religious depravity, and warns the Israelites not to emulate them. Saint Paul, in the Epistle to the

[3] Paul VI, *Address to Members of the Congregation of the Most Holy Redeemer* (September 1967), quoted in John Paul II, encyclical letter *Veritatis Splendor* (August 6, 1993), no. 80n131.

[4] John Paul II, encyclical letter *Veritatis Splendor* (August 6, 1993), no. 112.

[5] *Homily of His Eminence Cardinal Joseph Ratzinger* (April 18, 2005).

Romans, condemns the idolatry and sexual immorality of the pagan cultures of his own day. In general, the Church condemns the "false opinion which considers all religions to be more or less good and praiseworthy"[6] and teaches that "followers of other religions ... *objectively speaking* ... are in a gravely deficient situation in comparison with those who, in the Church, have the fullness of the means of salvation."[7] If some cultures can as a matter of objective fact be more deficient than others in the things necessary for salvation, then they can certainly be more deficient than others in the things necessary for economic prosperity and other worldly goods. Again, that does not mean that every disparity is justifiable. But it does entail that there is nothing "racist" or otherwise objectionable in explaining some disparities in terms of behavioral and cultural factors (such as family stability or instability, the value put on education, and so on).

Given the Church's teaching on homosexuality and the objective and complementary differences between men and women, she can also hardly accept the CRT position that traditional views about sexual morality, gender roles, and the like amount to "sexism", "homophobia", and "transphobia" and are therefore comparable to racism.

[6] Pius XI, encyclical letter *Mortalium Animos* (January 6, 1928), no. 2.

[7] Congregation for the Doctrine of the Faith, declaration *Dominus Iesus* (August 6, 2000), no. 22.

Despite a superficial overlap in a few of the themes emphasized by both Catholic social teaching and Critical Race Theory (such as the evil of racism and concern for the poor), CRT's basic vision of human nature and social life reflects a radical egalitarianism that is deeply contrary to natural law and Catholic moral theology.

If Catholic teaching is incompatible with CRT's diagnosis of social injustice, it is also incompatible with its proposed remedies. CRT writers such as Kendi advocate racial discrimination against whites and in favor of nonwhites. But the Church teaches that "any theory or form whatsoever of . . . racial discrimination is morally unacceptable."[8] The Church also teaches that "socio-economic problems can be resolved only with the help of all the forms of solidarity"—that is to say, of "friendship", "social charity", and "brotherhood".[9] By means of this solidarity, "tensions are better able to be reduced and conflicts more readily settled by negotiation."[10] By contrast, CRT writers reject the moderation of the traditional civil rights movement, emphasize securing power rather than changing minds via rational persuasion, and peremptorily dismiss as racists all those who would dare to disagree with them. They characterize social life as a conflict between

---

[8] *Compendium*, no. 433. Cf. *Catechism*, no. 1935.

[9] *Catechism*, nos. 1939 and 1941.

[10] Ibid., 1940.

inherently opposed racial interests rather than a partnership between friends or brethren. They increase social tensions by insisting that all whites be seen as complicit with oppression and interpreting all offenses as racist "micro-aggressions" and "implicit bias".

The 1988 document *The Church and Racism*, while calling for an end to the system of apartheid that then existed in South Africa, also warns against "racist reflexes on the part of the oppressed, which would be as unacceptable as those of which they are victim today" (9), and against "going so far as to replace violently one unjust situation with another injustice" (33). And it warns gravely against dehumanizing those accused of racism:

> In her denunciations of racism, however, the Church tries to maintain an evangelical attitude with regard to all. This is undoubtedly her particular gift. While she is not afraid to examine lucidly the evils of racism and disapprove of them, even to those who are responsible for them, she also seeks to understand how these people could have reached that point. She would like to help them find a reasonable way out of the impasse in which they find themselves. Just as God does not take pleasure at the death of a sinner, the Church aspires more to helping them if they consent to remedy the injustice committed. She is also concerned with preventing victims from having recourse to

violent struggle and thus falling into a racism similar to that which they are rejecting. The Church wishes to be a place for reconciliation and does not want to heighten opposition. She invites all to act in such a way that hatred be banished. She preaches love. She patiently prepares a change in mentality without which structural changes would be in vain. (27)

Nothing could be further from the paranoid, bitter, and vengeful spirit of Critical Race Theory.

As many of its critics have pointed out, if one were to replace expressions like "whiteness" and "white supremacy" with terms such as "Jewishness" and "Jewry", it would be difficult to distinguish CRT literature from the ugly propaganda of Nazism. Its claims are comparably extreme, even if it has not (yet?) led to comparable levels of violence. It also has manifestly totalitarian implications. CRT claims that racism permeates every aspect of human life, even into the unconscious motivations and seemingly innocent actions of individuals who suppose themselves not to be racist. It claims that any resistance to this CRT analysis is itself a manifestation of this omnipresent racism. It claims that it is not through rational persuasion, but rather only through the securing of power to enact policies that are extensive enough to eliminate every vestige of racial inequity, that this purported racism can be remedied. It claims that values like free speech, individual rights, color-blind policy, and the like are merely a smokescreen to hide the interests of "white supremacy". It claims that there are no neutral or objective criteria by which critics of CRT could show otherwise. It simply pits its own project of securing "antiracist power" against the forces upholding "racist power"—where the latter category includes anyone who dares to dissent from the CRT view of the world.

There is no way to implement this vision of the world without the sort of total control over society that National Socialists secured over German society and Leninist, Stalinist, and Maoist communists secured over Russian and Chinese society. As Pope Saint John Paul II warned in the encyclical *Centesimus Annus*:

> In the totalitarian and authoritarian regimes, the principle that force predominates over reason was carried to the extreme. Man was compelled to submit to a conception of reality imposed on him by coercion, and not reached by virtue of his own reason and the exercise of his own freedom. This principle must be overturned and total recognition must be given to the rights of the human conscience. (29)
>
> Totalitarianism ... in its Marxist-Leninist form, maintains that some people, by virtue of a deeper knowledge of the laws of the development of society, or through membership of a particular

class or through contact with the deeper sources of the collective consciousness, are exempt from error and can therefore arrogate to themselves the exercise of absolute power. It must be added that totalitarianism arises out of a denial of truth in the objective sense. (44)

CRT is grounded precisely in such a "denial of truth in the objective sense", and like Marxist-Leninist totalitarians, its proponents attribute to themselves a "deeper knowledge" of social reality which justifies them in taking "absolute power" by which they might impose their vision of the world by force rather than reason and an appeal to conscience.

Like Marxism and Nazism, Critical Race Theory cannot exempt religion from its totalitarian designs. Kendi pits "liberation theology" against what he labels "savior theology" and insists that the former alone is acceptable from the CRT point of view. He states:

Jesus was a revolutionary, and the job of the Christian is to revolutionize society ... to liberate society from the powers on Earth that are oppressing humanity ... That's liberation theology, in a nutshell. Savior theology is a different type of theology. The job of the Christian is to go out and save these individuals who are behaviorally deficient. In other words, we're to bring them into the Church, these individuals who are doing all of these evil, sinful things, and heal them. And save them. And then, once we've saved them, we've done our jobs... Anti-racists fundamentally reject savior theology, [which] goes right in line with racist ideas and racist theology.[11]

What Kendi labels "savior theology" and decries as a facilitator of racism is, of course, just basic traditional Christian theology. And the politicized reformulation of Christianity that he calls "liberation theology" has been condemned by the Church. Pope Saint John Paul II taught:

> This idea of Christ as a political figure, a revolutionary, as the subversive man from Nazareth, does not tally with the Church's catechesis... The Gospels clearly show that for Jesus anything that would alter his mission as the Servant of Yahweh was a temptation. He does not accept the position of those who mixed the things of God with merely political attitudes... The perspective of his mission is much deeper. It consists in complete salvation through a transforming, peacemaking, pardoning and reconciling love.[12]

Cardinal Joseph Ratzinger, who was prefect of the Congregation for the Doctrine of the Faith (CDF)

---

[11] "How to Be Anti-Racist: Ibram X. Kendi in Conversation with Molly Crabapple", held at Judson Memorial Church in New York City, August 15, 2019. Video of the event is available on YouTube, https://www.youtube.com/watch?v=BhbbmjqcRvY. Accessed October 2, 2021.

[12] *Address of His Holiness John Paul II* (January 28, 1979).

under John Paul II and would go on to become Pope Benedict XVI, warned that "the phenomenon of liberation theology ... constitutes a fundamental threat to the faith of the Church."[13] In 1984, Ratzinger's CDF issued, at Pope John Paul II's direction, an instruction criticizing the distinctive themes of certain so-called "theologies of liberation", bemoaning their "radical politicization of faith's affirmations" and noting that "some are tempted to emphasize, unilaterally, the liberation from servitude of an earthly and temporal kind. They do so in such a way that they seem to put liberation from sin in second place, and so fail to give it the primary importance it is due."[14] Particularly dangerous, the document notes, is the way liberation theologians adopt certain ideas from Marxism, and it singles out as examples the division of society into inherently hostile classes and the dogmatic tendency to dismiss all criticism as a smokescreen for the forces of oppression:

> It becomes very difficult, not to say impossible, to engage in a real dialogue with some "theologians of liberation" in such a way that the other participant is listened to, and his arguments are discussed with objectivity and attention. For these

[13] Joseph Cardinal Ratzinger with Vittorio Messori, *The Ratzinger Report: An Exclusive Interview on the State of the Church* (San Francisco: Ignatius Press, 1985), 175.

[14] Congregation for the Doctrine of the Faith, *Instruction on Certain Aspects of the "Theology of Liberation"* (August 6, 1984).

> theologians start out with the idea, more or less consciously, that the viewpoint of the oppressed and revolutionary class, which is their own, is the single true point of view. Theological criteria for truth are thus relativized and subordinated to the imperatives of the class struggle. (3)

It is hard to imagine a more perfect description of the mindset of Kendi and other apostles of Critical Race Theory.

Cardinal Ratzinger also warns of the naiveté of supposing that one can accept the basic Marxist conception of society as a struggle between inherently hostile groups while rejecting the rest of the Marxist system, for they are so conceptually interconnected that "if one tries to take only one part ... one ends up having to accept the entire ideology." In particular, the notion of "class-struggle" by no means merely entails social unrest of the kind every society exhibits, but "remains pregnant with the interpretation that Marx gave it" and entails "simplifications ... [which] prevent any really rigorous examination of the causes of poverty." Quoting a similar warning from Pope Saint Paul VI, Cardinal Ratzinger says:

> Marxism as it is actually lived out poses many distinct aspects.... However, it would be "illusory and dangerous to ignore the intimate bond which radically unites them, and to accept elements of the Marxist analysis without recognizing its

connections with the ideology, or to enter into the practice of class-struggle and of its Marxist interpretation while failing to see the kind of totalitarian society to which this process slowly leads."[15]

Exactly what such a society looks like is well-known to those familiar with the history of the Soviet Union, Maoist China, and other twentieth-century communist regimes. As Cardinal Ratzinger laments:

> Millions of our own contemporaries legitimately yearn to recover those basic freedoms of which they were deprived by totalitarian and atheistic regimes which came to power by violent and revolutionary means, precisely in the name of the liberation of the people. This shame of our time cannot be ignored: while claiming to bring them freedom, these regimes keep whole nations in conditions of servitude which are unworthy of mankind. Those who, perhaps inadvertently, make themselves accomplices of similar enslavements betray the very poor they mean to help.
>
> The class struggle as a road toward a classless society is a myth which slows reform and aggravates poverty and injustice. Those who allow themselves to be caught up in fascination with this myth should reflect on the bitter examples history has to offer about where it leads.[16]

---

[15] Ibid., no. 7. Quotation from Paul VI, apostolic letter *Octogesima Adveniens* (May 14, 1971), no. 34.

[16] Congregation for the Doctrine of the Faith, *Instruction*, nos. 10 and 11.

Such warnings lose none of their force when the concept of "race" is substituted for the concept of "class". Indeed, this substitution yields something reminiscent of the other main mass-murdering totalitarian ideology of the twentieth century, National Socialism. The moralistic pretensions of CRT writers should not blind us to this. As historian Claudia Koonz reminds us in her book *The Nazi Conscience*, Hitler's National Socialist movement did not regard its project as an evil one, and neither did many of those who observed or supported the movement in the years before it took power.[17] On the contrary, Nazism was claimed to represent a *moral* vision, and the claim was sincere even if delusional.

As Koonz notes, this vision had four main components. First, it understood ethnic groups in a collectivist rather than individualist way, seeing them as comparable to organisms of which the individual member is a part, and which can be either healthy or sick. Second, it was relativist, regarding what is good or bad as relative to an ethnic group, where the individual was expected to behave in a way that reflected solidarity with his own group rather than according to some standard outside the group. Third, it advocated a group's taking an aggressively oppositional stance toward other groups, particularly those seen as a threat to one's own group. Fourth,

[17] Claudia Koonz, *The Nazi Conscience* (Cambridge, Mass.: Harvard University Press, 2003).

it held that the legal system of a society ought to take account of the threat that one ethnic group is claimed to pose to another one, treating differently those citizens who are of the racial group seen as a danger to the other—as analogous to a "parasite" that endangers the health of its host. This vision was often presented in a dispassionate, matter-of-fact academic way, and it was taken to have communitarian moral implications that required a good person to behave in the interests of his group (ethnic Germans) and struggle against those groups claimed to pose a threat to it (such as Jews).

Though there are, of course, important differences between National Socialism and Critical Race Theory, it is disturbing how closely this characterization of "the Nazi conscience" parallels the CRT worldview. Again, if you substitute "white people" for "Jews" and "people of color" for "Germans", the resemblance is eerie. CRT writer Robin DiAngelo's relativist claims that "contrary to the ideology of individualism ... we represent our groups and those who have come before us" and that "we don't see through clear or objective eyes—we see through racial lenses" could have come straight from a work of National Socialist racial theory.[18]

---

[18] As Catholic social theorist Heinrich Rommen noted of racist theories of human nature like that of the Nazis, such theories maintain that it is not "the merits of objective reasons" that determine what the individual thinks and does, but rather "the inner subconscious voice of the blood, the race, etc." that does so; "the individual ... cannot

Her claim that "anti-blackness" is inherent to "white identity" parallels the Nazi view that Jews were inherently a threat to the health of the German nation. Ibram Kendi's rejection of color-blind policy and advocacy of discrimination echo the Nazi position that the state must treat its ethnic German and Jewish citizens differently. His comparison of purportedly omnipresent white supremacy to "stage 4 metastatic cancer" calls to mind the Nazi claim that certain races were "parasites" that threatened the health of the German people.

The Church has had to face down such malign delusions many times in her history. The political scientist Eric Voegelin argued that the twentieth-century totalitarian ideologies Marxism and National Socialism were modern heirs to the Gnostic heresy, which afflicted the early Church and reappeared in many different guises in subsequent centuries.[19] Critical Race Theory exhibits the same general features.[20] The Gnostic tendency is, first, to see

---

stand above these elements by force of reason, but is immersed in the inexorable current." *The State in Catholic Thought* (St. Louis: B. Herder, 1950), 75. This is hard to distinguish from the purportedly "antiracist" position of DiAngelo, Kendi, and other Critical Race Theorists.

[19] Eric Voegelin, *The New Science of Politics* (Chicago: University of Chicago Press, 1952).

[20] Cf. Edward Feser, "The Gnostic Heresy's Political Successors", *Catholic World Report*, January 31, 2021. Available at https://www.catholicworldreport.com/2021/01/31/the-gnostic-heresys-political-successors/.

evil as all-pervasive and nearly omnipotent, deeply enmeshed in the established order of things. For the early Gnostics, this evil order was identified with the reign of the God of the Old Testament; for Marxists, it is identified with capitalism; and for Nazis it is world Jewry. For CRT, it is "white supremacy". Second, the Gnostics held that only an elect who have received a special *gnosis* or "knowledge" from a Gnostic sage can see through the appearances of things to the underlying evil reality. For the early Gnostics, it was teachers such as Marcion, Mani, and other influential heresiarchs who passed along this *gnosis*; for Marxists, it is Marx, Engels, and other theorists who convey it; for the Nazis, it was Hitler. Critical Race Theory itself functions as a new *gnosis* that purportedly reveals to its adepts the unseen racial oppression they live under, with best-selling gurus like Kendi and DiAngelo functioning as modern Marcions and Manis.

Third, the Gnostics tended toward a Manichean division of the world into the forces of evil on the one hand, and on the other hand the "pure", who are armed with the *gnosis* to resist the evil forces in a great twilight struggle. (Indeed, the original Manichean heresy was precisely a variation on Gnosticism.) For Marxism this Manichean war is a struggle between the capitalist oppressor on the one hand, and the proletariat and its intellectual vanguard on the other; for Nazism, it is a war between world Jewry and its allies against the German nation led by the Nazi party; and for Critical Race Theory it is a conflict between "white supremacy" and "antiracism". Fourth, the Gnostics posited a final victory over this evil power, which entailed release from the material world, which the Gnostics saw as evil. Here is where the modern heirs of Gnosticism, which are materialist and see no hope for a life beyond this one, differ most radically from their ancient predecessor. (As Voegelin famously put it, they "immanentize the eschaton"—that is to say, they relocate the final victory of the righteous in this world and look forward to a heaven on earth.) For Marxists, this final victory will occur with the realization of communism; for Nazis, with the Thousand Year Reich; and for Critical Race Theory, with the destruction of "white supremacy" (along with "sexism", "homophobia", "transphobia", etc.).

Though claiming to pursue noble ideals, these variations on Gnosticism have spawned nothing but division, extremism, and worse. As Cardinal Ratzinger wrote, "It is ... painful to be confronted with the illusion, so essentially un-Christian ... that a new man and a new world can be created, not by calling each individual to conversion, but only by changing the social and economic structures."[21] Christianity cannot salvage these ideologies, for "by

---

[21] Ratzinger and Messori, *Ratzinger Report*, 190.

sacralizing the revolution—mixing up God, Christ, and ideologies—they only succeed in producing a dreamy fanaticism that can lead to even worse injustices and oppression."[22]

Catholics must resolutely oppose Critical Race Theory just as they have opposed these errors of the past—not *in spite of* being opposed to racism, but precisely *because* they are opposed to it. The Church's condemnation of racism is grounded both in our common nature as rational beings capable of knowledge and of charity, and in the redemption from sin made possible for all by grace. And this entails, not CRT's "cancel culture" and hermeneutics of suspicion, but rational discourse and mutual understanding. Not the demonization of any race as inherently oppressive, but solidarity and mutual respect. Not the endless ferreting out of ever more esoteric grounds for bitter grievance and recrimination, but the forgiveness and mercy that, as Pope Francis has emphasized, is "the true face of love".[23]

[22] Ibid.
[23] Francis, Angelus (July 14, 2019).

BIBLIOGRAPHY

Aquinas, Thomas. *On Kingship*. Translated by Gerald B. Phelan. Toronto: Pontifical Institute of Mediaeval Studies, 1949.

———. *Summa Theologiae*. Translated by the Fathers of the English Dominican Province. New York: Benziger Brothers, 1948.

Benedict XIV. Encyclical letter *Immensa Pastorum* (December 20, 1741). Reviewed in Panzer, *The Popes and Slavery*, and Eppstein, *The Catholic Tradition of the Law of Nations*, see below.

Benedict XV. Encyclical letter *Ad Beatissimi Apostolorum* (November 1, 1914). www.vatican.va.

Blankenhorn, David. *Fatherless America: Confronting Our Most Urgent Social Problem*. New York: Harper Perennial, 1996.

Bradley, Gerard V. and E. Christian Brugger, eds. *Catholic Social Teaching: A Volume of Scholarly Essays*. Cambridge: Cambridge University Press, 2019.

Chesterton, G. K. *The Defendant*. London: R. Brimley Johnson, 1901.

Church, Jonathan D. *Reinventing Racism: Why "White Fragility" Is the Wrong Way to Think about Racial Inequality*. Lanham, Md.: Rowman and Littlefield, 2021.

Crenshaw, Kimberlé, Neil Gotanda, Gary Peller, and Kendall Thomas, eds. *Critical Race Theory: The Key Writings that Formed the Movement*. New York: The New Press, 1995.

de Las Casas, Bartolomé. *A Short Account of the Destruction of the Indies*. New York: Penguin Books, 1992.

de Vitoria, Francisco. "On the American Indians". In *Political Writings*, edited by Anthony Pagden and Jeremy Lawrence, 231–292. Cambridge: Cambridge University Press, 1991.

Delgado, Richard and Jean Stefancic. *Critical Race Theory: An Introduction*. Third edition. New York: New York University Press, 2017.

DiAngelo, Robin. *White Fragility: Why It's So Hard for White People to Talk about Racism*. Boston: Beacon Press, 2018.

Engel, S. Morris. *With Good Reason: An Introduction to Informal Fallacies*. 3rd ed. New York: St. Martin's Press, 1986.

Eppstein, John. *The Catholic Tradition of the Law of Nations*. London: Burns, Oates, and Washbourne, 1935.

Eugene IV. Papal bull *Sicut Dudum* (January 13, 1435). www.papalencyclicals.net.

Feser, Edward. *Scholastic Metaphysics: A Contemporary Introduction*. Heusenstamm, Germany: Editiones Scholasticae, 2014.

Gregory XIV. Papal bull *Cum Sicuti* (April 18,1591). Reviewed in Panzer, *The Popes and Slavery*, and Eppstein, *The Catholic Tradition of the Law of Nations*.

Gregory XVI. Papal bull *In Supremo* (December 3, 1839). www.papalencyclicals.net.

Harrison, Lawrence E. *Who Prospers? How Cultural Values Shape Economic and Political Success*. New York: Basic Books, 1992.

Harrison, Lawrence E., and Samuel P. Huntington, editors. *Culture Matters: How Values Shape Human Progress*. New York: Basic Books, 2000.

John Paul II. Encyclical letter *Centesimus Annus* (May 1, 1991). www.vatican.va.

———. Encyclical letter *Veritatis Splendor* (August 6, 1993). www.vatican.va.

———. *Memory and Identity*. New York: Rizzoli, 2005.

John XXIII. Encyclical letter *Pacem in Terris* (April 11, 1963). www.vatican.va.

Kaufmann, Eric. *The Social Construction of Racism in the United States*. New York: The Manhattan Institute, 2021.

Kendi, Ibram X. *How to Be an Antiracist*. New York: One World, 2019.

Koonz, Claudia. *The Nazi Conscience*. Cambridge, Mass.: Harvard University Press, 2003.

Landes, David. *The Wealth and Poverty of Nations*. New York: Norton, 1998.

Leo XIII. Encyclical letter *Catholicae Ecclesiae* (November 20, 1890). www.vatican.va.

————. Encyclical letter *In Plurimis* (May 5, 1888). www.vatican.va.

————. Encyclical letter *Quod Apostolici Muneris* (December 28, 1878). www.vatican.va.

Lukianoff, Greg and Jonathan Haidt. *The Coddling of the American Mind: How Good Intentions and Bad Ideas are Setting Up a Generation for Failure*. New York: Penguin, 2018.

Nicholas V. Papal bull *Dum Diversas* (June 18, 1452). Examined in Raiswell, Richard. "Nicholas V, Papal Bulls of" in *The Historical Encyclopedia of World Slavery*, edited by Junius P. Rodriguez, Volume II, p. 469. Santa Barbara, Calif.: ABC-CLIO, 1997.

Osterweil, Vicky. *In Defense of Looting*. New York: Bold Type Books, 2020.

Panzer, Joel S. *The Popes and Slavery*. New York: Alba House, 1996.

Paul III. Papal bull *Sublimis Deus* (May 29, 1537). In Francis Augustus MacNutt, *Batholomew de Las Casas: His life, His Apostolate, and His Writings*. Cleveland: A.H. Clark, 1909. Internet Archive, https://archive.org/details/bartholomewdelas23466gut.

Paul VI. Apostolic letter *Octogesima Adveniens* (May 14, 1971). www.vatican.va.

————. Encyclical letter *Populorum Progressio* (March 26, 1967). www.vatican.va.

Pius X. Motu proprio *Fin Dalla Prima* (December 18, 1903). www.vatican.va.

Pius XI. Encyclical letter *Divini Redemptoris* (March 19, 1937). www.vatican.va.

————. Encyclical letter *Mit Brennender Sorge* (March 14, 1937). www.vatican.va.

————. Encyclical letter *Mortalium Animos* (January 6, 1928). www.vatican.va.

Pluckrose, Helen and James Lindsay. *Cynical Theories: How Activist Scholarship Made Everything about Race, Gender, and Identity—and Why This Harms Everybody*. Durham, N.C.: Pitchstone Publishing, 2020.

Pontifical Commission on Justice and Peace. *The Church and Racism: Towards a More Fraternal Society*. Vatican City: Pontificia Commissio Iustitia et Pax, 1988.

Pontifical Council for Justice and Peace. *Compendium of the Social Doctrine of the Church* (June 29, 2004). www.vatican.va.

Popenoe, David. *Life Without Father: Compelling New Evidence That Fatherhood and Marriage Are Indispensable for the Good of Children and Society*. New York: Free Press, 1996.

Popper, Karl R. *Conjectures and Refutations: The Growth of Scientific Knowledge*. New York: Harper and Row, 1968.

Ratzinger, Joseph Cardinal with Vittorio Messori. *The Ratzinger Report: An Exclusive Interview on the State of the Church*. San Francisco: Ignatius Press, 1985.

Rommen, Heinrich. *The State in Catholic Thought: A Treatise on Political Philosophy*. Providence, R.I.: Cluny Media, 2016.

Scruton, Roger. *The Need for Nations*. London: Civitas, 2004.

Second Vatican Council. Pastoral Constitution on the Church in the Modern World *Gaudium et Spes* (December 7, 1965). www.vatican.va.

————. Declaration on the relation of the Church with non-Christian religions *Nostra Aetate* (October 28, 1965). www.vatican.va.

Sowell, Thomas. *Discrimination and Disparities*. Revised and enlarged edition. New York: Basic Books, 2019.

————. *Intellectuals and Race*. New York: Basic Books, 2013.

Tierney, Brian. *The Idea of Natural Rights*. Grand Rapids, Mich.: William B. Eerdmans Publishing Company, 2001.

Urban VIII. Papal bull *Commissum Nobis* (April 22, 1639). Reviewed in Panzer, *The Popes and Slavery*, and Eppstein, *The Catholic Tradition of the Law of Nations*, which see.

Voegelin, Eric. *The New Science of Politics*. Chicago: University of Chicago Press, 1952.

Walton, Douglas. *Informal Logic: A Pragmatic Approach.* Second edition. Cambridge: Cambridge University Press, 2008.

Wilson, James Q. *The Marriage Problem: How Our Culture Has Weakened Families.* New York: HarperCollins, 2002.

INDEX